End

Morgan's powerful b_ _ _ _ through our children is full of revelation from Scripture, wisdom in knowing how to walk out that revelation, and stories of personal experience in raising and training her own children. You will receive much inspiration and encouragement as you embrace the task of raising your children to be the people God has called them to be. We highly recommend her well-written, insightful book!

    Jim & Lisa Anderson
    Founders of Sexuality Unmasked
    Authors of *Yes to Motherhood* and *Unmasked*

*****

Morgan's vulnerability and authenticity are displayed on every page of this cutting-edge, practical guide for the modern-day parent. *Spirit Seeds* is inspirational! There are practical parenting tips on almost every page for those who are feeling overwhelmed, distraught, or who think that they are failures as parents. There is hope. The author's personal stories and illustrations act as a potential lens for the reader to peer into his or her own life and adventures, either as a parent or as one who takes care of children and teens. This moving story will shock you but also prepare you for this challenging journey called Life.

    Dr. Stan Fleming
    Gate Breaker Ministries
    Author of *Gate Breakers, Pathways,* and *Allah Weeps*

*****

It is with joy that I recommend Morgan Stigall's first book, *Spirit Seeds*. Her humble, sweet, and beautiful self is present in every page, and as you read her stories woven with Scripture, you will be inspired and encouraged. Morgan shares relatable experiences in parenting with a touch of humor and a great deal of heart and humility. She doesn't share a list of rules for being a successful parent. Rather, she imparts fresh vision and insight for nurturing, loving, and caring for the precious children God has given to us. This book is an excellent choice for individual or small-group study. The questions at the end of each chapter will encourage meaningful and open discussion that will help parents to support one another in their journey. Truly, you will be inspired!

> Kathleen Fleming
> Grandmother, teacher
> Author of *Joan and the Fish*

*****

Spirit Seeds is rich with Scripture and teaches you to lean in to God, hear His voice, and do what He says. A great reminder to be God's warrior for your children. Both mothers and fathers can highly benefit from applying the principles in this book.

> Ruben Mundo
> Worship leader, Rock Church City Heights

Morgan provides practical strategies for parenting God's way through funny, relatable stories. From the introduction I felt the Holy Spirit moving and encouraging me in how I raise my children. I was crying before I reached page 1. This book is a must-read.

> Amy Mundo
> Content Coordinator/Script Writer, Rock Church San Diego

Spirit Seeds

A Warrior's Guide

to

Raising an Army

Morgan Stigall

Copyright

Spirit Seeds – A Warrior's Guide to Raising an Army

by Morgan Stigall

Copyright © 2020 by Morgan Stigall

All rights reserved. This book is protected by the copyright laws of the United States of America. This book may not be copied or reprinted for commercial gain or profit. The use of short quotations or occasional page copying for personal or group study is encouraged. Permission will be granted upon request from Morgan Stigall.

Scripture quotations marked NKJV are from the New King James Version, © 1982 by Thomas Nelson, Inc. Used by permission.

Scripture quotations marked NASB are taken from the New American Standard Bible, © 1960, 1962, 1963, 1968, 1971, 1972, 1973, 1975, 1977, 1995 by the Lockman Foundation. Used by permission.

Scripture quotations marked NIV are taken from the New International Version, © 1973, 1978, 1984, 2011 by Biblica, Inc. Used by permission of Zondervan.

Scripture quotations marked ESV are from the English Standard Version of the Bible, © 2001 by Crossway Bibles. Used by permission.

ISBN: 9798654461278
Published by SPRING MILL PUBLISHING
Sharpsburg, Maryland 21782 USA
Editing/Layout by Jim Bryson (JamesLBryson@gmail.com)
Graphics by Amani Hansen (NoBoxez@Yahoo.com)

Dedication

TO MY AMAZING CHILDREN who have taught me far more about Jesus and His love than any adult ever could. You all are such a beautiful representation of our Lord. Thank you for teaching me to serve and love more than I ever thought possible. Our time together is something I will always treasure deep in my heart. You inspire me.

Contents

Foreword xiii

Introduction xv

Beginnings xvii

1. Foundations 1
2. Abraham 9
3. Faith and Hearing 25
4. In Jesus We Discipline 37
5. In Jesus We Build 59
6. Weeding and Warring 75
7. For and With 95
8. My Crucible Moment 107
9. Childhood's End 133

About the Author 139

Acknowledgements

THE WORDS I WRITE HERE will never be able to express the depth of my gratitude for what I've received. I am abundantly blessed with so many amazing people that have poured into the person that I am today. I feel like this book is a compilation of the several times that the Lord jumped up inside me in the middle of conversation during fellowship to shout, "Pay attention! This is what I have to say about that!"

With all that I am, I give my God glory! He makes the broken new, and the unqualified qualified in an instant. He puts dreams in our hearts and sees them through. I am everything because of Him and nothing without Him.

A giant THANK YOU to:

Travis, my best friend in the world and amazing husband. He has been my steady support and encouragement throughout this whole book process, even throughout our marriage! He fights for truth, loves and serves steadily and faithfully. Quietly, in the unseen, he wars for those who never know it. He is a man. I am honored to walk beside him, go to war with him, stand behind him and serve with him.

My children, Judea, Eden, and Selah, who have stepped up the chores, waited patiently while I finished a thought, and are allowing our lives to be on display for all who read! They've invited others to see their shortcomings, struggles and strengths, all with a joyful heart! Thank you for all of your time and sacrifice! I know that this hasn't been easy!

For all the moms that have gone before me! My mother, Le Whitehead and mother in-law, Carol Stigall, I have learned so much from you both! I am so grateful to be able to glean from all you have sown and harvested. You've taken such good care of me. You have shown me what kind of mom I want to be, what kind of grandmother as well. I admire you both. You've given me more than I could ever thank you for.

Mom, you've been there for me and supported me for my whole life, sometimes despite your preference. You made it clear that you were for me! I could always count on you to go to battle for me. You were always my biggest cheerleader!

Carol, thank you for laying a firm foundation; it was no easy task! You brought me in and called me daughter when you didn't even know me. You have taught me so much about the love of Christ, being a Christian, and loving my husband and children!

A big thank you to my spiritual mama: Bobbette Moss. You were there any time I had a question, a random thought to bounce off of you, or a concern. You coached me through births of babies and ministries. You have been such a source of wisdom and hope for me!

Thank you to my friends and sisters in Christ: Tara Hendershott, Lisa Arndt-Stigall, Naphtali Morden, Amanda DeLand, Ericka Gregston, Sandy Espinoza, Terri West, Suzanne Brooks, Amy Mundo, Kelli Youk, Sarah Holmes, and Ruth Erickson. Thank you for bringing me into your homes and pouring into me all that you had, for sharing your lives and families and wisdom with me! Thank you for listening to my countless questions, for spending time reading and giving me feedback! Thank you for believing in me and investing in my family!

Thank you, Dess Butler, Trisha Cooper, Jessica Anderson, and Chelasea Mills, for being my prayer warriors. Our times together have been rich!

To my sister, Michelle Ells, I love you! Thank you for believing in me and being my forever friend. No matter what, I know I have you!

Stan and Kathleen Fleming, for believing in Travis and me and raising me up from a babe! Thank you for your grace! Candy Craddick, Candice Williams, and Kathy Cole for always having that little bit I needed in the moment, for being steady and strong, for fighting for my family in prayer!

To our pastors and friends: Jeff and Robie Ecklund, Joel and Lindsey Ecklund, thank you for teaching truth unapologetically. Thank you for stirring the church and not allowing her to grow stagnant, for stirring my heart and dreams!

Brian and Cindy Dockins, thank you for leading with truth and love and for walking through this life with me. You are my spiritual parents. I know that I can go to you with whatever I have and you will bring wisdom, truth and love. You've taught me so much!

Cynthia Williamson, my sweet niece for taking my photos, for speaking every word that God puts in your heart, and being such a fire starter!

All of you have loved me like family. You have been family. You are my friends. You have helped to weave the dreams and ideas for this book just by being who you are! It is from our times of fellowship that the Lord has pulled from and used to shape every weapon of truth in this book.

Jim Bryson, this book literally wouldn't be published without you. I am in awe of the wisdom and discernment the Lord has given you. You have poured into me in ways I never expected. I have grown so much in this short season of editing! Thank you for encouraging me and speaking life and truth!

Amani Hansen, thank you for praying over and designing my cover! What an amazing gift you have, what an amazing gift you are!

To my friends: My God has blessed me with too many amazing people to possibly thank! My good friends, I love you! Know you are in my heart when I say thank you! Many of you have spoken over me, believed in me, and have encouraged me in this process. Thank you, I hope you know who you are! You are so dear to my heart and I love living life with you in it!

May God bless you all!

Foreword

By Pastor Jeff Ecklund

ALL AROUND US, WE SEE LIFE STARTING IN SEED FORM. Flowers, trees, ideas, dreams, even human life, all begin as seed. Children are our most precious seed, and they need careful cultivation. If you want to affect their spiritual development, you should start when they're young. This begins with training—not for them, but for you.

Spirit Seeds is a good place to start, itself a seed to raising a spiritual army. It is transparent and challenging, offering feedback for reflection and a clear pathway toward the adventure of Christian parenting in a modern world. *Spirit Seeds* will make you laugh and cry as it provokes you with concrete insights and direction—a real help to your endeavors to raise up your children in the way they should go. *Spirit Seeds* builds on solid biblical foundations, blending the importance of faith and discipline with the author's personal experiences in personal warfare for herself and her family. As strong as it can be in parts, however, there is no "lording over" in this book. Morgan Stigall is as real as it gets. She's been in the trenches and has learned how to fight her way out. As you experience Spirit Seeds, you will learn as well.

I've anticipated this book from the moment Morgan started writing. I actually pressed and pushed for it. Why? Because Morgan Stigall is one of the most unique people I know. She is gifted, personable and charismatic. One of the things I appreciate about Morgan—something she is famous for—is her laughter! And yet those who only see her lighter side might miss the warrior spirit that burns within. In truth, it is the strongest among us who can afford to be the most gracious. If law and order married mercy and grace, you would have Morgan.

As her Pastor and friend for lo, these many years, Morgan has been a joy to walk with. If you can't meet her in person, the next best thing is to read her book, *Spirit Seeds*, and discover the treasures of her insights, critical thinking and dependency on the strength of God for victory in her and her children's lives.

Reading *Spirit Seeds* is a lot like raising children; it is deep and easy and ultimately rewarding. You won't be disappointed. *Parents: You need to read this book!* Your children need you to read this book. The Kingdom of God needs you to read this book.

...for the Kingdom of Heaven belongs to such as these.

Introduction

But the fruit of the Spirit is love, joy, peace, patience, kindness, goodness, faithfulness, gentleness, self-control; against such things there is no law.

Galatians 5:22

WELL, THAT'S GREAT, APOSTLE PAUL, but how do I fully live in the Spirit and its fruit? More so, how do I teach my kids the same? And how do I even attempt this without being a hypocrite?

I don't know about you parents out there, but half the time I am a hot mess who is barely holding it together. More times than not, I have looked at the adorable face of my child in sheer frustration, thinking to myself, *I don't know what to do with you!*

Praise God for the Holy Spirit! Thank you, Jesus, that we can come to You with every need.

God has given me a gift—the truth and reality of how quickly children grow up. He's given me the perspective to choose to enjoy and live fully in the moment, whether it be chaos or peace. Kids grow up so fast. Life truly is a vapor, and this season of life called parenthood is so short. I'm honored to have the privilege of raising His children. It humbles me.

In this book, I will share the story of how God led me to sow into my children, reaping a harvest that was worth the exhaustion of the plowing and sowing seasons.

I want to start by clarifying that my husband and I don't have it all together. We definitely don't know everything about parenting. I don't have a Ph. D. in child psychology. My picture has never been on the cover of a family magazine.

I don't have all the answers. I don't have a secret formula. What I have is the prompting of the Holy Spirit and all He has shared with me throughout my years of youth ministry and parenting—revelations that have forever changed me and my family.

Jesus asked me to write this book. Apparently, the things He has instilled in my heart for my children are not just for our family.

I believe wholeheartedly that this book is from Jesus to you. The Lord wants you to know that you have the ability to hear Him with clarity. He has a plan that He wants you to know about. He chose you to be your kids' parents. He didn't make a mistake. He opens and closes the womb. Your children were not an "accident." (See Genesis 29:31, 1 Sam. 1:5) He has given me life-changing revelations that hack the roots of the flesh: "immorality, impurity, sensuality, idolatry, sorcery, enmities, strife, jealousy, outbursts of anger, disputes, dissensions, factions, envying, drunkenness, carousing and things like these..." (Gal. 5:19-21).

I don't have the answers, but Jesus does. He has given me insights into raising kids that produce good fruit. A good orchard is such a blessing, but a lot of work to prepare!

Allow me to take you there.

Beginnings

I MET JESUS ON OCTOBER 10, 2000. I will never forget meeting Him for the first time. I had heard about Him but never knew Him. I grew up in a home where we were taught there was a God, He lived in Heaven, and that's where dead people went.

I was 18 years old when I dedicated my life to Jesus. Coincidentally, I had been dating the same boy, Sean (not his real name), for close to three years and was sure I'd marry him. I thought I loved him, at least as I understood love, but I didn't know true love until the day I let Jesus into my heart.

Jesus began shaking my world, and nothing would ever be the same again. He was healing and teaching me His ways about so many things. Then came a big change. Six months into my walk with Jesus, He said that I was not strong enough to continue seeing Sean. God was so merciful to me, but it was time to set some things right. He said *enough* to the sexual temptations flowing from this immature and impure relationship.

I was wrecked. I loved this boy. In my head, Sean was everything—my world, my future, my life. I couldn't comprehend living without him. But God's word was clear: "I have something better!"

Although I loved God, I was angry. It was the first time God's word actually hurt me. I was afraid to obey, but I did.

Then I made a deal. I asked God that if He really had something better, to give me six months with just me and Him to get to know each other before He gave me my spouse. Looking back on it, six months was a ridiculously short time; of course, I was ridiculously young. But I'd never been without a relationship.

I'd gone from boyfriend to boyfriend since kindergarten. Six months unattached to a guy seemed like an eternity.

I struggled after the breakup. Suddenly single, I didn't know who I was. Well, I didn't really know Jesus either, and I was still looking for love in all the wrong places. Yet in all my mistakes, God trained me and held me close.

Sean was also devastated. We wept together. I knew why we couldn't be together, but he didn't understand. It broke my heart. I didn't know how to communicate Jesus with him. How could I say that "something better" doesn't mean "you are not good enough," but instead meant "you are not right for me, but more than enough for the Lord"?

We muddled our way through trying to be friends. Sean begged me to come back. I was sick inside. I wanted to, but I knew I'd be disobeying the Lord.

Two months later, at his birthday party, I broke down and asked him to get back together. As the words left my mouth, however, I felt the grief of the Holy Spirit imploring me: "But I have something better!"

My heart ached, but I didn't want *better*. I just wanted this pain to end and my friend whom I loved to stop hurting. I didn't know any other way to do this.

In October, six months from the day I'd broken off our relationship, God began to press into my life with greater urgency. I sensed that this was about more than Sean; it was a choice between spiritual life or death. Every day that I lived in disobedience, I felt greater pain than when I'd separated from Sean. I hated being a liar. I was torn.

I hated myself for disobeying God, and so much more for putting this poor, unsuspecting, unknowing boy that I thought I loved in the middle of my disobedience. Instead of alleviating his pain, I was making it worse.

Just as obedience to God brings life and blessing to more than just yourself, disobedience to God brings pain to all those around you.

God continued his gentle pressure on me. Finally breaking down, I prayed like Jesus in the garden, "Take this cup from me, if there be any other way."

I finally broke it off the relationship with Sean again. This time, although I felt awful for the poor guy that I had dragged through the disaster of my disobedience, I felt so much better. I was at peace. I knew that in the long run, Sean would be better off as well. Who wants to marry someone running from God's will?

The next morning found me spending time with God. Ever the drama queen, I was telling Him that I'd never get married, that I was certain I'd be an old maid. Years from now, they'd write songs about the old lady who lived alone in a shack. Oh, the hilarious, fatalistic perspective of an 18-year-old girl!

That's when God sweetly interrupted my lament.

"You already know him."

"WHAT?!"

God is *so* good to interrupt our vanity and speak truth into our spirits.

"He's been in front of you this whole time."

"*Who* has?"

"Travis is your husband."

"Whoa, hold on, God. This is CRAZY! Didn't I just break up with Sean? What are you doing?"

It got crazier.

God told me that Travis knew I was his wife. He already knew! That freaked me out. I kept thinking, Do I really hear you right, God? This is too much.

Sunday arrived and guess who always gave me a ride to church? Yup, Travis.

I was a nervous wreck. Now, at that time of my life, I was the kind of person who couldn't keep from saying whatever I was thinking. I felt fake or a liar if something relational needed to be declared but was not. So, when Travis came to the door, I flung it open and exclaimed: "I know what you know!"

He didn't even get to say "Hello." He just paused, eyed me suspiciously, and then walked nonchalantly to the car, saying over his shoulder "No, you don't."

Naturally, I persisted.

"I know what you know!"

The blindsided Travis could only reply, "No you don't."

I insisted that I did, and that's where we left it until we went to youth group that night. Apparently, while the night was in full swing one of my friends told him the news that I had finally broken up with Sean for good. So, I no longer had a boyfriend.

Well, one thing about Travis—he is quite serious and isn't one to dilly dally. He's a realist. I had been dating Sean for three and a half years, so Travis and I never even thought of having a date. Suddenly, on our way to take me home, he had his opening. This was his big chance to pour forth all that was in his heart, to share everything God was doing, to begin laying the foundation of our future life together. He had to make it good.

"I like you."

"You *like* me? What does '*you like me*' mean, Travis?"

I knew what he knew, but I wasn't going to make it easy on him. Besides, I was freaking out—excited and scared and so weirded out.

"You don't know what I know," he replied.

This was fast becoming an awkward car ride.

"Yes, I do," I said, "and you better pray and make sure it's ok with God that you tell me."

He prayed and got quiet for a minute. Even though I knew what Travis was going to say, when his words broke the sound barrier, my heart leapt.

"God told me that you're my wife."

"Shut up!" I laughed. "He told me that you're my husband."

So it was, two days after I obeyed and broke up with my boyfriend of nearly four years (with a short break in there), God gave me my husband. I was beyond shocked! I actually heard God speak! It was not in my head. This was real! And my life was forever changed.

Later, God told me to look at my calendar. I got it out with my journal, and He showed me that if I had obeyed and never got back together with Sean, I would have had six months to the day alone with Jesus, just He and I before He gave me my spouse—exactly the time I wanted.

Oh, my heart!

I had asked God for something, and He not only showed me that He hears me and has plans that are better than mine, but that He longs for obedience... for my growth, for my benefit, and for the benefit of others. So many hurts inflicted on my ex-boyfriend and his family could have been avoided, and Jesus' reputation protected, had I listened and obeyed completely. I learned a lot of painful lessons there.

God loves us so deeply. Who gets their spouse that way? I do apparently. And what a man I got!

Travis and I decided that since we were getting married, a date might be a good idea. We went on our date, were engaged in December and married in August the following year.

Now, as of this writing, my amazing husband Travis and I have been married for 17 years. We have three beautiful kids and God has written such a beautiful story.

He is a great author.

Let's get started.

1

Foundations

God Is in the Details

AS PARENTS, WE LAY THE FOUNDATION for our children's lives. Their habits and core values will mostly be formed from our lifestyle—what we teach and live day to day at home. The key is to know who you are in Christ, be an obedient child yourself, and the rest will follow.

God has a plan for each of our lives, and that includes our children's lives.

> *Your eyes have seen my unformed substance; And in Your book were all written the days that were ordained for me, when as yet there were none of them. How precious also are Your thoughts to me, Oh God! How vast the number of them!*
>
> *If I should count them, they outnumber the sand.*
>
> Psalm 139:16-18

When your first child arrived, you probably experienced the wallop of reality that you are a parent and responsible for keeping your child alive. You probably sat there as the title of "parent" sunk in, wondering about tomorrow with a worrisome tilt to your heart.

Perhaps you were a nervous reader like I was. A deep planner. You were going to be the parent who did things *this way* or *that way*, and definitely not *any way*. I read so many books! I had to know what to expect in labor and what the best was for my baby. I had to know what the healthiest *everything* was. I was going to be the perfect mom. I wanted to raise well-behaved, clean, healthy children. Don't we all? But I was going to make it happen. I was going to do everything right even if it killed me.

Oh, my poor husband and son. I could have been diagnosed OCD. I allowed the enemy to steal the joy of the Lord and His rest from me. I tried to control everything. I worried constantly and compared myself to other moms. Still, it was all with the heart of bettering myself to serve the Lord and my family. I had so many ideas of how to do this wife/parent thing—there was a right and wrong way for everything. I was going to do it right... all the time!

Sadly, I was looking in the wrong places. What I needed couldn't come from comparisons to other people. I needed the Lord's leading. I needed to parent with an eternity-based mindset. We all do. We need to live that way. We need to store up our treasures in heaven. Today, I want nothing more than for my children to walk in God's will and spend eternity with our King. Nothing else matters more. Yet to accomplish that, I have to live that... Every. Single. Day.

I need to know God's plan for my life. I need to be an obedient child. I need to listen well and obey completely. I cannot earn my place in heaven—it's already assured—but I can enjoy a life of rich blessing, abundance and peace that God wants for me and my family.

In studying God's Word, I find that the key to good fruit is obedience. I know that our God longs to give us good gifts. He wants us to prosper. He wants blessings to transfer and grow from generation to generation. For my children and grandchildren to receive this grand inheritance, I have to do something. I must obey.

There is a striking word in the Bible that I encounter over and over—*if*.

If you love me, keep my commandments.

John 14:15

If you know these things, blessed are you if you do them.

John 13:17

If...

If we obey, if we listen, if we do what He asks, many promises are fulfilled for blessing and fruit. If we do not obey, listen and do, the Lord is sure to correct us. Our goal is to be Christlike, and that begins with faith, and faith works through obedience and action.

> *Beware of the false prophets, who come to you in sheep's clothing, but inwardly are ravenous wolves. You will know them by their fruits. Grapes are not gathered from thorn bushes nor figs from thistles, are they? So every good tree bears good fruit, but the bad tree bears bad fruit. A good tree cannot produce bad fruit, nor can a bad tree produce good fruit. Every tree that does not bear good fruit is cut down and thrown into the fire. So then, you will know them by their fruits. Not everyone who says to me, 'Lord, Lord,' will enter the kingdom of heaven, but he who does the will of my Father who is in heaven will enter. Many will say to Me on that day, 'Lord, Lord, did we not prophesy in Your name, and in Your name cast out demons, and in Your name perform miracles?' And then I will say to them, 'I never knew you; depart from Me, you who practice lawlessness.'*

Foundations

Therefore everyone who hears these words of Mine and acts on them, may be compared to a wise man who built his house on the rock. And the rain fell, and the floods came, and the winds blew and slammed against that house; and yet it did not fall, for it had been founded on the rock. Everyone who hears these words of Mine and does not act on them, will be like the foolish man who built his house on the sand. The rain fell, and the floods came, and the winds blew and slammed against that house; and it fell-and great was its fall.

Matthew 7:15-27 NKJV

According to the Word, faith is shown through obedience, and merely doing good deeds just to do them is lawlessness. To be considered wise, one must act on what the Lord says; the one who does not act is a fool.

I have learned many lessons about obedience through motherhood. I can't count the times when correcting my kids that the Lord has whispered, "Oh really? And does this apply to you also?"

Let me share a few stories from my home that the Lord used to reshape my thinking.

ORDER UP!

Our house was on the market and I received a call to show it. The people were due to arrive in 30 minutes. My daughter, Eden, needed to clean her room. It was a disaster, so in the loving tones of the calm, collected Christian mom, I told her, "Go clean your room right now." To the others, I hollered "All hands on deck!!! Get this place sparkly clean and fast!"

Foundations

We'd sold a house once before and the kids knew the drill. This wasn't their first rodeo. However, instead of cleaning up, my lovely Eden thought to herself, *Mom hasn't eaten this morning, and she's working really hard. I'm sure she wants breakfast.* So instead of obeying my orders, she decided to surprise me with a meal.

Five minutes before we were due to evacuate the premises, as I was putting the vacuum away, I received word that breakfast was served.

Breakfast? Oh no...

The freshly cleaned kitchen looked like Julia Child just lost a food fight with James Beard. It was a disaster, and Eden's room still looked like WWIII. I knew my little one's heart was to help. Her beaming face said it all. Unfortunately, all I could register at that moment was gritted teeth and a forced smile: "Thank you, Eden. Clean your room now. I've got to clean up this mess in the kitchen!"

Of course, I knew that if the house was to sell, it would sell, mess or no mess. But as I pondered what to do next time, the Lord spoke to me: "It's not the intent; it's the act of obedience that brings blessing."

See, I can do nice things for Jesus all day long, but if I'm not doing what He asked me to, am I really helping the kingdom? Or does God have to clean up my well-intended messes? Is my motive to truly please him? Or to do what I think will please him?

God has a big picture in mind and eternity for all who will believe. He knows what others need to gain salvation and He wants us to be a part of the process. When we let our children help us build something, they take ownership in it.

How often do we slave over things and end up feeling unappreciated, torn, weary, exhausted and futile? That is not God's portion for us. He wants us to have life and have it abundantly. He longs for us to work hard and rest well. He wants us to serve joyfully.

> *There is nothing better for a person than that he should eat and drink and find enjoyment in his toil. This also, I saw, is from the hand of God*
>
> Ecclesiastes 2:24

The secret is to do what He asks. Of course, there will be times when you do something simply because it's the right thing to do, and sometimes there will be great and painful sacrifices, but that is not all the time. Truly, God will ask you to do specific things and to focus your efforts on those specific things. Obeying will honor Him, increase the Kingdom, and do more than all of your nice, random ideas to help God. I've learned with children who don't have the bigger picture in mind, that unasked-for help is not always helpful at all. Has your child ever dumped half a bottle of laundry soap in the washer? Put your expensive hang-dry-only dress in the dryer on high? Cut her sister's hair to save you money?

Of course, they're kids. The intention was good but it wasn't what you asked for. In the end, their work, their effort, was not only wasteful but harmful to your goals.

Here's one more.

I told my son, Judea, to do the dishes before I got home from work. Unfortunately, he disobeyed me and everyone had to wait for dinner. We live in a tiny house, and I literally can't cook dinner in our kitchen with breakfast and lunch dishes on the counter. Judea's disobedience negatively affected everyone in the house.

Everyone had to wait for dinner, and soon the whole house was irritable.

However, if Judea would have obeyed and done the dishes when I had asked, the whole house would have been blessed! He wouldn't have had to do his chore with an irritated mom hovering over him, rushing him along. Instead, we would have experienced a joy-filled evening with fellowship—time spent over a hot meal cooked with love and joy.

Obedience and disobedience affect others no matter what the intention.

THE STRUGGLE

Perhaps you are in the heat of a struggle. Perhaps you compare yourself to other parents, constantly beating yourself up for not being what you think you should be. Perhaps you have so many ideas of what you should be that your mind won't let you be content in the moment. You are at constant war with yourself, trying with all your might to make it all happen. Perhaps you are reading every book you can find to live up to what you should be, to produce the best kids you can, to be the best parent, best spouse, best Christian, best child... Perhaps you always feel that you fall short just like I did. Your intentions are good but are you being obedient? Are you doing what you were asked or are you trying to do more?

Sweet friend, let me encourage you. You are enough! God picked you! He picked you and your spouse and no one else to be the parents of your children. He knows your innermost parts (ref. Psalm 139). He designed you for this. He's got it. He will not let you go.

Foundations

Hold on, take a breath, and know that your kids are His kids. God is faithful and will not give up on you. Listen in. He will speak to you about your children. He adores them. He created them as the fruit of your union with your spouse. He has a plan and purpose for their lives and for your life.

God is in the details. In every Bible story I read, I see great detail given in areas of instruction. Do you think it'd be different with you and raising your kids? Do you think He'd give you children, create purpose for their lives, count the hairs on their heads and not instruct you in raising them?

Perhaps you're incredibly frustrated and feeling hopeless. In the back of your mind, you're saying to yourself, "I didn't plan for children. I didn't ask for this!"

You might not agree with this, but I hope you read on anyway. God opens and closes the womb. You or your significant other conceiving this child is by no means an accident! God has a plan and a purpose for both you and your child!

A man's heart plans his way, but the Lord directs his steps

Proverbs 16:9

Behold children are a gift from the Lord, the fruit of the womb is a reward.

Psalm 127:3

We often have our own ideas for our lives, our hopes and dreams. Often, we think God is messing up the plans we have, or we fear that He will. But our God is a good, a good Father, and He longs to give us good gifts from the desires of our hearts. As we grow in Him, our desires will naturally change shape and become His desires.

2

Abraham

THE WORD OF GOD IS LADEN with great stories that serve as examples of how we're supposed to parent. Not only that, but we have Holy Spirit to guide us in raising our children. So, anything that brings us close to Holy Spirit also leads us into better parenting.

Each child is different; each one needs different attention and guidance. We can't (or shouldn't) do the same thing with each child and expect the same result. God made us individuals. This is why He communicates with us individually. Each of us is unique, just like everyone else. So are our children.

The Word has many examples of people who were living life their own way until God spoke promise and direction, changing their lives forever. Abram (later, Abraham) is an excellent example.

We first hear of Abram in Genesis 12, when God calls him out of his country and promises him great things.

> *The Lord said to Abram: "Get out of your country, from your family and from your father's house, to a land that I will show you. I will make you a great nation; I will bless you and make your name great; and you shall be a blessing. I will bless those that bless you, and I will curse those that curse you; and in you all the families of the earth shall be blessed."*
>
> Genesis 12:1-3 NKJV

God is great at getting our attention and changing our life course to a direction we would have never thought of ourselves.

Abram was 75 years old when he left his homeland of Haran. God spoke new identity and life into Abram and set a promise into his heart. Naturally, at age 75, the promise of nations for his future children had to seem a bit far-fetched, yet he departed Haran in obedience to God.

OBEDIENCE AND DOUBT

How important do you think Abram's obedience was for *his* future? How important do you think Abram's obedience was for *our* future?

Imagine receiving such an exciting, heavy word. In a sense, you already have. Through Abram, nations were birthed. Through you, blessing and cursing can come to your children and your children's children. Through you, a foundation is either laid or destroyed. It is a mighty calling to be a parent. It is not a task to be taken lightly.

Abram obeyed and left his homeland. I'm sure he was excited about his calling from the Lord and the promise still fresh in his heart. It must have been easier to obey with God's intense promise still fresh within him—through him that all of the families of the earth would be blessed. Crazy stuff!

Abram arrived at the place God had for him and the Lord confirmed it. Abram built an altar for the Lord and called on His name, then continued traveling. He traveled to Egypt because the famine in the land was severe.

Reading the story stirs my imagination. I picture what it would have been like to be Abram, to be called the father of generations. I imagine the grandeur and weight of such a promise. The responsibility would rest heavily on my shoulders. I imagine that Abram was depressed when he found famine in the land God had promised him.

Hardship wasn't promised, only great blessing. Did he wonder if he had correctly heard God? Was doubt whispering ever so softly while fear made sharp jabs at his shield of faith?

Abram knew God called him, but as doubt in himself and his ability stirred—he never doubted God—fear disturbed his decision-making skills and natural leadership. As he and his wife, Sarai, grew closer to Egypt, he worried that he would be killed by a jealous Pharaoh because of Sarai's beauty. His promised land didn't look the way he expected. Famine wasn't in the promise. Hardship wasn't mentioned either. Only big, awesome blessings.

Did I really hear God?

Abram had a very real battle with self-doubt, and it whispered a fear-based, self-reliant plan in Abram's ear (ref. Gen. 12:10-20).

I'm not sure if Abram was truly worried about his life or if he felt it was up to him to protect God's promise. Either way, he took it upon himself to guard his own life instead of covering his wife and trusting God. He put Sarai in a very awkward position, perhaps without even realizing it, because of fear.

The fear of man is one of the enemy's favorite tools to use against God's chosen. Abram had it all—land, a beautiful wife, a mighty promise from God! Yet as soon as hardship came, he made some regrettable decisions. Doubting himself, he grew weary in the process, and that doubt stirred and twisted his understanding of God's promise.

MOSES AND INFERIORITY

In doubting ourselves and our own ability to do what God called us to, we're still doubting God. In doubting ourselves, we're doubting God's design. God shows this to us with Moses. God spoke life and promise into Moses, yet Moses questioned God. He doubted that he had what it took to do what God was asking him to do.

> But Moses said to God, "Who am I that I should go to Pharaoh and that I should bring the sons of Israel out of Egypt?
>
> Exodus 3:11

Moses and God went back and forth, and then in Exodus 4:1 Moses said, "What if they will not believe me or listen to what I say?"

Patiently, the Lord affirmed Moses, giving him signs and wonders to perform, yet at the end of all that, Moses was still struggling with doubt.

> But Moses said to the Lord, "Oh, my Lord, I am not eloquent, either in the past or since you have spoken to your servant, but I am slow of speech and of tongue." Then the Lord said to him, "Who has made man's mouth? Who makes him mute, or deaf, or seeing, or blind? Is it not I, the Lord? Now therefore go, and I will be with your mouth and teach you what you shall speak." But he said, "Oh, my Lord, please send someone else." Then the anger of the Lord was kindled against Moses...
>
> Exodus 4:10-14

It's never a good thing when the anger of the Lord is kindled against you. That's a sure sign that you've pushed things a bit too far.

God knows the plans He has for us (ref. Jerimiah 29:11) and He wants us to fulfill them. God wasn't mad at Moses because Moses was the only person who could do what He wanted. God can always find someone who will go. No, God was mad because He has hopes and dreams for each of His children and He longs to see us walk in our full potential. God was mad because He designed Moses, raised Moses, and knew he'd be perfect for this job.

OBEYING GOD

Obeying God doesn't always make sense in our own mind. Obeying usually means we have to walk in something that makes us uncomfortable and quite possibly will make us look stupid to other people (especially if God doesn't show up). Those are the tasks that build our faith and the Kingdom of heaven.

Let us return to the story of Sarai (later Sarah), Abram's wife. As Abram feared, she was noticed right away by the princes of Pharaoh. Abram said she was his sister so they wouldn't kill him and take her. Instead, the princes commended her to Pharaoh and she was taken into his house. Sarai obeyed her husband and went along with the lie, saying that she was his sister.

Imagine what she felt! Do you think she felt honored and protected by her husband? Not hardly. Still, she was not alone in history. Men and women of the Bible, chosen to lead generations in the ways of God, were often knocked off course when fear and doubt came in! Thankfully, even though Abram feared and doubted the process of fulfilling God's promises, God kept His

Word. God said He'd curse those who curse Abram and bless those that bless him.

True to his Word, God afflicted Pharaoh and his household with great plagues while Sarai was there. Pharaoh knew something was askew and returned Sarai to Abram. Pharaoh was understandably upset about Abram's lies, yet he sent them on their way with all he had.

As Abram left Pharaoh's house, he was probably feeling humbled by the realization of what he'd done. He had been reminded of who God is and nudged in the direction he should have been going in faith. After this incident, Abram traveled back to his tent, his land and the altar he made for the Lord. He took all he had, including his nephew Lot.

With a great revelation of God's nature fresh in Abram's mind, he began to show himself a man of integrity. It wasn't long before it was tested again. When the land could no longer support both Abram and Lot, bickering broke out amongst their people. Abram wanted peace and allowed Lot to have the first choice of the land available.

Lot was self-focused, prideful and young. He chose for himself what looked like the better land—the land that was sure to elevate him to a higher status than his uncle. However, Abram was steadfast and didn't waiver in character despite Lot's immaturity, and God blessed Abram for it.

Once Abram was settled into his new land, God reminded him of His promise. God challenged him to walk confidently in the promise he received. God gave him the land, and his descendants would be too many to count! Again, a reminder of the promise and a long season of waiting.

Abraham

About 15 years later, a war broke out. It was four kings against five. Lot was taken as a prisoner of war. Even though Abram and Lot had been separated, when an escaped servant ran to Abram pleading for help, Abram gathered all of his men and servants, armed them, and went to rescue Lot. In so doing, he chose to be a man of honor. He chose to be valiant and fight for family.

I can't stop thinking about the time gap: 15 years and he still had none of the children God promised. None!

God once gave me a big promise. It's only been five years, yet I have often struggled, doubted and whined. I know God is big enough, but I sometimes doubt the process. I wonder if I am enough. I know God is enough, but what about me? My pride is in not believing He made me enough. He is good, and He reminds me of that, but I am in awe of Abram's strength to keep on going for all those years of hardship! His story spurs me on, reignites my faith, renews my mind and infuses me with hope!

Abram's fight to get Lot back won the entire war! At that time, Melchizedek was the king of Salem. Melchizedek was so thrilled that the war had been won that he blessed Abram, and Abram gave him a tithe of all he had. Abram was also offered riches from the King of Sodom who wanted him to give over the people in exchange.

> *And the king of Sodom said to Abram, "Give me the persons, but take the goods for yourself." But Abram said to the king of Sodom, "I have lifted my hand[c] to the Lord, God Most High, Possessor of heaven and earth, that I would not take a thread or a sandal strap or anything that is yours, lest you should say, 'I have made Abram rich.' I will take nothing but what the young men have eaten, and the share of the men*

who went with me. Let Aner, Eshcol, and Mamre take their share."

Genesis 14:17:24

Abram refused the riches offered to him because he told the Lord that he would take nothing. This was a small act of Abram's faith, but it showed the Lord that he trusted Him and that he was starting to believe he was who God said he was. Abram knew that God deserved all the glory for everything that he owned. There is so much power in that! So much blessing!

God pursues Abram even more.

At this point in Abram's life, he was essentially going through the motions—acting on what he knew God wanted but receiving little day-to-day revelation from God. After the separation from Lot, and through the subsequent wars, the Bible doesn't mention any deep conversations between Abram and God. As such, Abram was a man with an unfulfilled promise and a fleeting hope. He had to have wondered: *How? When? Will God's promises ever be fulfilled?* I'm sure in the depths of Abram's heart there was a profound doubt: *What if I heard wrong?*

Enter God:

But after these things the word of the Lord came to Abram in a vision saying; "Do not be afraid, Abram. I am your shield, your exceedingly great reward."

Genesis 15:1 NKJV

Abram answered God with a heart cry:

Lord God, what will You give me, seeing I go childless, and the heir of my house is Elieser of Damascus?

Genesis 15:2

Abram cried out! I imagine him on his knees, yelling and weeping, "God, are you who you say you are? Why is this taking so long? Where is my promise?"

> *And behold the word of the Lord came to him saying, "This one shall not be your heir, but one who will come from your own body shall be your heir. Then God brought him outside and said, "Look now toward heaven and count the stars if you are able to number them," and he said to him, "So shall your descendants be."*
>
> Genesis 15:4

I LOVE this!!! God tells him to go outside so that he can communicate with him more clearly and in a way he would understand. God uses pictures, creation, and so many other things to get our attention.

> *The heavens declare the glory of God, and the sky above proclaims his handiwork.*
>
> Psalm 19:1

God longs for us to know Him and His plan for us, and He will keep trying, reminding and pursuing us until we get it right, because He loves us so much. God has done this with me more times than I can count, and He will do this for you. If you will listen and obey.

Abram went on and asked God to reassure him. God gave him a prophetic dream, one with much detail and instruction. Notice the process: Abram asked; God answered... again and again. Of course, he was still tempted to hurry things along a bit, to do everything he could to make the promise happen. The story of Abram and Sarai is a great lesson in trusting God's process.

ON OUR OWN

Ever since the fall of man, we all struggle with this specific temptation. In our desire to please God, we try to gain our gift in our own power and timing. In so doing, we try to control our circumstances to force into existence the promises God gave us. I see this in myself, my husband, my kids, and those to whom we minister. We all stumble over this same log again and again. Admitting it makes it almost laughable, but we all do this with regularity.

Abram fully trusted God and was pretty solid in knowing the promise was going to take time. But Sarai still doubted. She was unsure. Sarai and Abram talked about what God was doing, but Sarai had her own ideas of how this was supposed to play out. It was taking longer than she pictured. I think Sarai felt responsible that she wasn't producing children. Back then, if a woman was barren, culturally it was always her fault. I believe she felt awful, blaming herself for her husband not becoming the man God promised him to be. The guilt probably ate at her. She must have felt responsible to do something that God hadn't mentioned to receive this promise.

Sarai was ready to see God's plans fulfilled. This promise didn't make sense any other way, so she offered her maid Hagar to bear Abraham's child, something that was culturally acceptable. She did what she thought she had to do to obtain the promise. Yet nowhere in scripture did she check with God first.

Is that what God wants? Is that anywhere in scripture as an example to us? No! God always gives clear instructions on what He expects. She could have simply asked instead of assuming.

However, she thought of a plan—something she could control, and she took action. Just like Adam and Eve, Sarai gave to her husband, he took, and another fall was born.

The interaction between Sarai and Abram is a message to couples walking through God's promises. Abram was ready to walk fully, however long it took to trust God, but Sarai had an idea. Yet Abram was also culpable in this deed. He stumbled by heeding his wife's voice and taking Hagar into his bed.

Ladies, we have got to pray and seek God before we bring ideas to our men! We have got to make sure it is God's idea and not our own! We are more naturally the home organizers, the schedulers, the detailed ones who get things done.

The lesson here is to make sure you ask the Lord before setting forth on a course of action, even if it appears to be the direction in which the Lord said you'd be heading. The consequences could last for generations.

Thankfully, God is so merciful, and poor Hagar, who was used and abused throughout this process, was looked after by the Lord who heard her affliction and rescued her and her son.

We really don't know much about Hagar except that she was Sarai's maidservant. How did she feel about her place in life? Did she long to be like Sarai with promises of God whispered throughout the land? Did she long to be free, known, and married? Was she already jealous? Did she willingly go into Abram's bed hoping to take Sarai's rightful place? Did she go in with something to prove to Abram? Or, was she forced, feeling it her duty, embedding a root of bitterness into the walls of her innermost parts?

Abraham

Whatever the case, Hagar conceived and it is still a lesson to us today. The strife in the Middle East has its root in the fruit of Hagar's womb, Ishmael. He is the father of their people.

Oh, but our God is good, faithful, and merciful! Today, the sons of Ishmael are literally having the Lord appear to them! He's calling out to them to save them and God is being glorified! In the midst of war and chaos, peace is stirring because of the promises of Jesus. God desires that none should perish.

Ishmael is proof that not waiting on God's timing and making your own plan has its consequences. It's also proof that when we don't follow His path, He will use the hard things for great lessons. He is merciful. There was a plan for Ishmael, even if to Abram and Sarai it only looked like a bad situation. God brings beauty from ashes.

God knows where you are. He knows when people sin against you, and He will correct them here on earth or in eternity. He will discipline them. Likewise, when we sin, when we try in our own strength to gain the promise on our own, there will be consequences that affect not only our lives but anyone connected with our lives. We will be corrected. We will face uncomfortable, sometimes heart-wrenching consequences. But God is faithful. He is just. He is a good, good Father.

Even though Abram and Sarai tried to make things happen in their own strength, and life-changing things came about as a result, God didn't give up on Abram. He called him out again.

I am Almighty God; walk before Me and be blameless.

Genesis 17: 1

The Lord reminded Abram of who He said he was supposed to be, refreshing the promises between them. To make His point and renew him to a deeper degree, the Lord even renamed him. He was now called Abraham.

LESSONS LEARNED

This story reveals much.

- It shows us how God gives identity and speaks promises and big plans for our future.
- It shows the importance of direct obedience and how fear tries to make its way into our hearts to lead us off the safe path God has chosen for us.
- It shows how integrity is honored and brings favor from the Lord.
- It shows how, when we try to control the timing and conditions of our promises, the Lord is faithful and just to discipline us and redirect our paths. Those attempts to elevate ourselves into God's promises don't go unnoticed.
- It shows us that God never gives up on us... even in our failures. He is willing to re-speak identity, truth and life into our futures and renew the promise in our hearts.
- It shows God's ability to change the world through a baby and a family, and that He plans our lives in love and hope.
- It shows that when we fall short, He is willing to redirect us and use our shortcomings and mistakes to bring glory to His name. Notice how God continued to speak to Abram even after he did things in his own way. God continued to seek Abram out, to interrupt his life-mess and speak new life into him.

Abraham

Whatever difficulties you are in, God wants to speak to you about your future. He wants to give you direction and promise. He wants to guide you, speak life into you, and walk with you through this life.

Life might not be the way you pictured. The road might look different than you expected. The barren, muddy field with no fruit is just the beginning. Soldier on, my friend. The future is bright. God's timing is perfect. Fruit trees take hard work and time to start producing.

Raising children is no different. God will speak to you. He will direct you, bless you, and show you the path to abundant life. The question is:

Are you willing to listen?

Abraham

DISCUSSION QUESTIONS:

1. Where are you in your relationship with Jesus?
2. Do you hear Him speak to you? (Let me encourage you to watch one the best teachings I've heard on hearing God's voice. In fact, without understanding this concept, the next chapter will be irrelevant to you. Dess Butler: How to Hear God's Voice)
3. What promises do you have stirring in your heart?
4. In what ways have you tried to make those happen on your own?
5. What do you need to surrender to allow God to retake His rightful place in bringing His plan for your life to fruition?

3
Faith and Hearing

CHRISTIANITY TELLS US THAT GOD IS A TRIUNE BEING—a Father, Son and Spirit. Of the three, it is frequently the Holy Spirit of God that we hear when God is speaking to us.

Hearing the voice of God is something everyone on the planet has done whether they recognize it or not. Some call it their conscience, some talk about "the little angel on our shoulder" arguing with the little devil on their other shoulder. Regardless of how people describe it, God speaks, and it's up to us to learn to listen to Him... or not.

When it comes to the voice of God, it's important to know one thing—it's personal. God desires to have relationship with us and to communicate with us through the Holy Spirit. He longs to visit with us, spend time with us, and yes, even tell us what we need for the day.

Have you ever had a time when you thought that you had better do something, then when you didn't do it, you suffered the consequences?

One fine summer day as I walked out the door, I felt strongly that I should grab my umbrella. However, when I looked out at the clear blue sky, I denied that sense and didn't think twice about it until later when the sky darkened, the clouds opened and rain poured on my sunny disposition. At that moment, I realized it was the Holy Spirit that I had heard telling me to bring my umbrella. I had ignored God's voice. It sounded the same as so many other things He often shared with me, but I never thought he would speak about such a small issue as weather protection. And yet he does. He cares so much about the tiny details of our lives! Other than keeping me dry, He was training me to listen to the little things because that's how we get to know Him well enough to listen to the big things.

FAITH

Faith, according to Hebrews 11:1, is "the substance of things hoped for, the evidence of things not seen." To have faith, in essence, means you believe without seeing, but you have evidence to do so.

God wants you to know Him well enough that He can speak a word and you will listen and obey. Not because He wants to force you into slavery, but because He wants you to be safe and have a life free from sin, failures, and mistakes that may cause pain for you and others around you. (Remember the story of Abram and Sarai, from our previous chapter.)

To be a person of faith means what? Does it mean that you simply believe in God? Or does it mean that you believe God is who He says He is and that He will do what He says He will do?

The Bible says:

By grace you have been saved through faith; and that not of yourselves, it is a gift of God; not as a result of works, so that one may boast.

Ephesians 2:8-9

Let that sink in: *We are saved through faith.*

Scripture goes deep into teaching about righteousness through faith and what it means to live by faith. And for good reason. We have to understand faith to walk with the Holy Spirit.

Without faith, we won't listen to Him. Without faith there is no hope. Without faith we quite literally cannot move forward.

So, let us go into the book of Romans, talk more about our renamed man and what this might look like. Take a moment and pray before you read this passage, and ask the Holy Spirit to speak to you through it.

> *But now God has shown us a way to be made right with him without keeping the requirements of the law, as was promised in the writings of Moses and the prophets long ago. We are made right with God by placing our faith in Jesus Christ. And this is true for everyone who believes, no matter who we are.*
>
> *For everyone has sinned; we all fall short of God's glorious standard. Yet God, in his grace, freely makes us right in his sight. He did this through Christ Jesus when he freed us from the penalty for our sins. For God presented Jesus as the sacrifice for sin. People are made right with God when they believe that Jesus sacrificed his life, shedding his blood. This sacrifice shows that God was being fair when he held back and did not punish those who sinned in times past, for he was looking ahead and including them in what he would do in this present time. God did this to demonstrate his righteousness, for he himself is fair and just, and he makes sinners right in his sight when they believe in Jesus.*
>
> *Can we boast, then, that we have done anything to be accepted by God? No, because our acquittal is not based on obeying the law. It is based on faith. So we are made right with God through faith and not by obeying the law.*
>
> *After all, is God the God of the Jews only? Isn't he also the God of the Gentiles? Of course he is. There is only one God,*

and he makes people right with himself only by faith, whether they are Jews or Gentiles. Well then, if we emphasize faith, does this mean that we can forget about the law? Of course not! In fact, only when we have faith do we truly fulfill the law.

Abraham was, humanly speaking, the founder of our Jewish nation. What did he discover about being made right with God? If his good deeds had made him acceptable to God, he would have had something to boast about. But that was not God's way. For the Scriptures tell us, "Abraham believed God, and God counted him as righteous because of his faith."

When people work, their wages are not a gift, but something they have earned. But people are counted as righteous, not because of their work, but because of their faith in God who forgives sinners. David also spoke of this when he described the happiness of those who are declared righteous without working for it:

> *"Oh, what joy for those*
> *whose disobedience is forgiven*
> *whose sins are put out of sight.*
> *Yes, what joy for those*
> *whose record the LORD has cleared of sin."*

Now, is this blessing only for the Jews, or is it also for uncircumcised Gentiles? Well, we have been saying that Abraham was counted as righteous by God because of his faith. But how did this happen? Was he counted as righteous only after he was circumcised, or was it before he was circumcised? Clearly, God accepted Abraham before he was circumcised!

Circumcision was a sign that Abraham already had faith and that God had already accepted him and declared him to be righteous—even before he was circumcised. So Abraham is the spiritual father of those who have faith but have not been circumcised. They are counted as righteous because of their faith. And Abraham is also the spiritual father of those who have been circumcised, but only if they have the same kind of faith Abraham had before he was circumcised.

Clearly, God's promise to give the whole earth to Abraham and his descendants was based not on his obedience to God's law, but on a right relationship with God that comes by faith. If God's promise is only for those who obey the law, then faith is not necessary and the promise is pointless. For the law always brings punishment on those who try to obey it. (The only way to avoid breaking the law is to have no law to break!) So the promise is received by faith. It is given as a free gift. And we are all certain to receive it, whether or not we live according to the law of Moses, if we have faith like Abraham's. For Abraham is the father of all who believe. That is what the Scriptures mean when God told him, "I have made you the father of many nations." This happened because Abraham believed in the God who brings the dead back to life and who creates new things out of nothing.

Even when there was no reason for hope, Abraham kept hoping—believing that he would become the father of many nations. For God had said to him, "That's how many descendants you will have!" And Abraham's faith did not weaken, even though, at about 100 years of age, he figured his body was as good as dead—and so was Sarah's womb.

Abraham never wavered in believing God's promise. In fact, his faith grew stronger, and in this he brought glory to God.

He was fully convinced that God is able to do whatever he promises. And because of Abraham's faith, God counted him as righteous. And when God counted him as righteous, it wasn't just for Abraham's benefit. It was recorded for our benefit, too, assuring us that God will also count us as righteous if we believe in him, the one who raised Jesus our Lord from the dead. He was handed over to die because of our sins, and he was raised to life to make us right with God.

Romans 3:21-4:25 NLT

Wow! I know that's a lot of information. Let's break it down.

Abraham heard God's voice, listened and obeyed in faith. Even when it seemed ridiculous, Abraham believed. He couldn't see the future. He didn't have a plethora of signs and wonders to prove what he heard was God. Remember, he even fell short, stumbled and had to learn to trust that he was who God said he was. All Abraham had to go on was a small, quiet voice that he had tested and trusted. Abraham knew who was speaking and he learned to take God at His word. The results were profound.

- Because he had faith, he was justified.
- Because he had faith, his sins were forgiven.
- Because he had faith, it was counted as righteousness.
- Because he had faith, he became the Father of many nations.

We can work for God until we're exhausted, but until we listen, believe it is truly Him and obey, we are at best good people with good intentions trying to be enough for heaven yet justified by nothing. We need to remember that we work out our salvation with fear and trembling (ref. Phil. 2:12). We need to trust God, and yes, even fear (or revere) God enough to obey when we don't fully understand and cannot see the complete outcome.

I know that is a heavy word, but God did not say we get to heaven by works. In fact, He said something quite different: we get to heaven by faith proven through works.

What is faith without works? Consider this from James:

What good is it, my brothers, if someone says he has faith but does not have works? Can that faith save him? If a brother or sister is poorly clothed and lacking in daily food, and one of you says to them, "Go in peace, be warmed and filled," without giving them the things needed for the body, what good is that? So also faith by itself, if it does not have works, is dead.

But someone will say, "You have faith and I have works." Show me your faith apart from your works, and I will show you my faith by my works. You believe that God is one; you do well. Even the demons believe—and shudder! Do you want to be shown, you foolish person, that faith apart from works is useless? Was not Abraham our father justified by works when he offered up his son Isaac on the altar? You see that faith was active along with his works, and faith was completed by his works; and the Scripture was fulfilled that says, "Abraham believed God, and it was counted to him as righteousness"—and he was called a friend of God You see that a person is justified by works and not by faith alone. And in the same way was not also Rahab the prostitute justified by works when she received the messengers and sent them out by another way? For as the body apart from the spirit is dead, so also faith apart from works is dead.

James 2:14-26 ESV

Faith and Hearing

To some, this might seem elementary; it's a common teaching. I have heard it often. Yet this word refreshes my soul because my soul needs to be reminded. This "faith and works" practice is about intimate relationship with Jesus—to know Him well enough to ask, listen and do. I can read my own words and be encouraged because I long to know Him more. Indeed, He's ministering to me even as I write this. I need to remember that I am not an accident. Further, God did not make a mistake in giving me three beautiful children to raise. I need to remember what it means to have faith when He asks me to do something big and scary like share my deepest thoughts with the world! I too need to hear Him say, "Good job, Morgan! I chose you for such a time as this."

You have to have faith; you cannot earn your way into the Kingdom of Heaven. Did your child have to earn their way into the womb? Did they have to work before you provided a home for them? A bed in your house? NO! They are your children. You provided for them because they're yours. You want the best for them. You "made" them in your act of marriage. (Or, in your act...) We know God made them, but in our hearts, those children are ours. Similarly, God wants you as His, not because you earned it but because He made you as His. He has provided for your entire life. He wants more for you. All you have to do is trust Him like a child... just like your children trust you.

If you hear God speak and don't believe it's Him, then you don't really believe at all. That's the point. To have faith is to step out into something that you hope for. Again, when we listen to God in the minor things, the major things will come easier. There will always be evidence that it is Him. Deep down, you'll know, but it'll be scary and new and will seem a little wild. Fun, huh?

Faith and Hearing

Try Him out. Next time you feel that nudge of the Holy Spirit to grab your umbrella on a sunny day, do it and see what happens. He wants you to get to know Him. He'll prove himself in the small things and change your life in the big things.

All of this faith and trust translates into our children—how we raise them and what they become. God made our children as individuals, each one different from their parents and from each other. He knows what they need to feel loved. He knows what they need to be disciplined. He knows what they need to grow up with the identity that they are His sons and daughters. He wants them to know that they have worth, purpose and a reason to be on this planet. He also wants this for you.

He will not fail you. He will speak to you about your kids. He will tell you when to keep your mouth shut, when to hug a little longer, when to not fear and get some sleep, when to pray a little harder, when to help and when to let them learn the hard way. He will be by your side the whole time.

He will not fail you.

We will fail, but His grace is sufficient, and in Him we will be enough.

LISTEN – TRUST – OBEY

Leaning in and listening to the Lord for your children might look and sound different than it does for me. Again, we are all individuals. The Lord speaks to me according to my personality and relationship with Him. He knows what words will get my attention. For example, I know He speaks more directly to me than he does to a more tender-hearted friend of mine. When I shared a word that God spoke to me in correction, she was shocked. "That could not have been God; He is not that harsh!"

But I knew it was Him. I would have never turned and repented if He had been more tender in His words to me. My friend needs a gentle nudge. I need a steel wedge splitting green hickory. We are different daughters with different needs.

Children are the same way. Some will need more structure, instruction and firmer boundaries reiterated often, while others only need a gentle word and boundaries already looser than their own standards. Some need to hear "tighten up!" while others need "loosen up!"

We as parents have to pay close attention to how our children were created. We need to look into their personalities and parent accordingly. When praying for our children, we need to ask God specifically to show us how to grow each one. Different types of plants need different care to flourish; likewise, our children.

Prayer is two-way conversation. Study it, spend time learning God's voice. The more you do, the more you will be able to recognize His voice in regards to your children.

Here is an example from my life. My girls loved *My Little Pony*. In that show, the ponies have a saying, "Cross my heart, hope to fly, stick a cupcake in my eye." This reminded me of a childhood saying I grew up with: "Cross my heart, hope to die, stick a needle in my eye."

Once I grew up enough to think seriously about what that meant, I found it disturbing. Then one day, the Holy Spirit jumped up inside me when the girls repeated the Pony saying in play. He led me to sit with my kids and come up with a saying of our own, a family motto of sorts. This is what we came up with, and honestly, we should not get credit because it was totally the Lord.

Faith and Hearing

> *Trust the Lord, do your best,*
> *Know that grace covers the rest.*

That is much better than a cupcake in the eye. It conveys God's promise over whatever situation we're facing.

Let's face it—life is hard. We all fall short of the glory of God. We all stumble, we all fall, we all doubt from time to time, and we miss it. We try and try, yet often in our own strength. This saying re-centers everything. It brings us back to the great news: We have Jesus! He is enough. If we trust Him, if we listen and obey, it will all work out!

In our moments of failure and shortcoming, we repent and ask for forgiveness. His grace is enough for us. We will learn and grow. Our kids will learn and grow with us, and a healthy foundation of hope, faith and love will be laid.

CHAPTER DISCUSSION QUESTIONS:

1. In what ways have you heard God's voice and are just now recognizing it as Him?
2. Do you feel faith is more important now that you have children? Why or why not?
3. Have you ever "missed it?"
4. How did you know you missed it?
5. What did you learn from that incident and how have you grown because of it?
6. How will you apply hearing the Holy Spirit to your daily life from now on?

4

In Jesus We Discipline

BUCKLE YOUR SEATBELTS, PARENTS. Instructing our kids in how to love and obey the Lord is not up to our friends, pastors or those gifted to teach. It is up to us. Let's learn to do it well.

Draw near to God, and He will draw near to you.

James 4:8

Scripture tells us that the fruits of the Spirit are these: love, joy, peace, patience, kindness, goodness, faithfulness, gentleness, and self-control (ref. Galatians 5:22-23) It is with these qualities that we live, discipline, lead and teach our children. The promise is that in our toil of training, good fruit will eventually come. As we work to prepare the ground and sow good seeds, God waters with our love, our words, our time and our consistent discipline applied in the fruit of the Spirit.

Sounds perfect, right? So, how are you doing in applying these qualities? And what results are you getting? If you're like most of us, you see a mixture—some good, some not so good, as you and your spouse strive to do your best.

Welcome to normality!

Now, how to make our best better?

THE WAR OF OUR LIVES

Take a moment to absorb this reality: Our lives are on stage for our children. They learn from what we do, not from what we say. It's a hard truth sometimes, especially when we look at our children and see a reflection of ourselves that reveals more than we anticipated. The truth is, our kids model what they see in us. When we see good fruit, it's lovely, but facing the not so pretty sides of ourselves is never easy.

That is why it is vitally important that we soak in the Spirit of the Lord, so that when we pour out our best efforts, our fruit will bear His likeness and be filled with that which waters us. Want spirit-filled kids? Water yourself with the Word. Be connected to the vine, which is Jesus, and allow Him to be your life source (ref. John 15:1-17).

It's difficult to watch my kids struggle with insecurities because I've battled with insecurity. It's wrenching to watch my kids deal with a perfectionist mentality because I battled that for years. Sometimes I trip over what the enemy planted years ago just when I thought I had it all weeded out. I've been freed, but the weeds had already entangled the trees in my orchard. It's painful to see someone I love so much hurt because I didn't recognize the enemy in my camp.

Praise God that He points the enemy out to us! Praise God that His grace is sufficient! Praise God that HE WINS! But it doesn't mean the work is easy. It means the work is fruitful. We need to be diligent watchmen. We need to tend our orchards with a fierce response toward any enemy trying to enter and rob us. We need to protect our children with our lives—for they are our lives. We need to wage war, though not the way the world does.

> *For though we walk in the flesh, we do not war according to the flesh, for the weapons of our warfare are not of the flesh, but are divinely powerful for the destruction of fortresses. We are destroying speculations and every lofty thing raised up against the knowledge of God, and we are*

> *taking every thought captive to the obedience of Christ, and we are ready to punish all disobedience, whenever your obedience is complete.*
>
> 1 Corinthians 10:3-6

We as parents—indeed, as humans—need to be aware of the very real war going on for our souls and the souls of our children. Thoughts that do not align with the Word of God must be expunged from our minds. We must wage war against anything that would try to raise itself above the Lord. We must instantly recognize the battle for what it is.

This includes the vanity mindset of having well-behaved, clean, healthy children on display so it looks like we have our lives together. Appearances are the wrong motivation. In Deuteronomy 6:4-9, God commands us to love the Lord our God with all our hearts, souls and might. Then He tells us to teach his commands diligently to our children.

> *Hear O Israel! The Lord is our God, the Lord is one! You shall love the Lord your God with all your heart, with all your soul, and with all your might. These words, which I am commanding you today shall be on your heart. You shall teach them diligently to your sons and shall talk of them when you sit in your house and when you walk by the way and when you lie down and when you rise up. You shall bind them on your hand and they shall be as frontals on your forehead. You shall write them on the doorposts of your house and on your gates.*
>
> Deuteronomy 6:4-9 NASB

The commandment from the Lord to teach our children is an ongoing commission requiring diligence and regularity. Every moment with our children should be intentional. I'm not talking about over-spiritualizing everything and making every single minute a lesson about Jesus. I'm saying recognize that every breath is an opportunity to show your child to whom they belong and what it means to be a son or daughter of God—present and listening to the Holy Spirit. Be ever listening; turn your ear toward God! Victory can only be won by the faithful. Indeed, the key to freedom and favor for both our children and ourselves is obedience. Obedient children are trusted children. They are given more responsibilities, more freedom and frankly, more time to enjoy life.

Like many of us, I grew up knowing there was a God in heaven who watched everything I did. I had heard of Jesus and that He "loved" me... from far away. It was a good start for my budding theology, but the reality is that Jesus wants to sit with us in the same room and share our lives. He wants to enter the rooms of our hearts and heal our wounds, erase all the pain that life brings so He can fill us with joy and peace regardless of our circumstances.

Yet God gave us free will. He is a gentleman. He will not force us to do anything. He wants the best for us, but He will not invade what we do not surrender. This is why discipline is so important. We are not slaves; our children are not slaves. Sons and daughters discipline themselves to follow their Father. Discipline is a function of the will, and when necessary, it is applied as correction from the top down.

DISCIPLINE BRINGS PEACE

Discipline is a controversial topic today, yet its foundation is laid out clearly in God's word. So while this next verse may stir up some deep emotions, keep reading. Let it unfold. God is loving and purposeful. Every scripture has a purpose.

For the Lord disciplines the one he loves, and chastises every son whom he receives

Proverbs 13:24

I know that to show love to my kids, I need to discipline them, teach them the ways of God, and truly live Jesus day in and day out, moment by moment. I must lead.

Children need leadership. They are not mature enough to handle themselves without healthy boundaries and guidance. Yes, even preteens and teens need a leader. They need to learn how to handle extreme emotion and deal with it appropriately. They need to learn to obey without fear. But to do so, we as parents must provide consistency.

Too often, we parents fail to set clear boundaries. We struggle to provide sufficient guidance or give a clear picture of right and wrong, perhaps because we are not certain ourselves. Generally, our boundaries are moved by what is convenient at the time.

Too often, we allow our fatigue, our mood, our hormonal imbalance or daily circumstances to govern what we can handle and where our boundaries are set. We are inconsistent and yet we expect steadfast peace and obedience. Is it no wonder that we have chaos?

The fact is that kids are incredibly smart. They learn quickly that boundaries are changed by emotional circumstances, and they will begin to manipulate your emotions to get you into a state of loose boundaries. If you think I am wrong—if you don't believe kids are that smart—go sit at the mall play area and watch how toddlers work their exhausted parents. Do you want to be a puppet with your child on the other end of the strings, or do you want to lead and guide your child to a life of abundance in the Lord?

We comfort ourselves with the lie that chaos comes from these little ones not fully understanding. We make excuses for their behavior. *They don't really understand. They're too young to learn.* The truth is, they really *do* understand. It's we parents who don't.

Using an extreme example, consider neglected children in third-world countries who forage for food, fight for survival and work harder than many adults. At a basic level, they understand the system they live in and become masters at obtaining what they need. Now, if kids with malnourished bellies and undeveloped intellects can function at such a level of complexity, then your children can understand simple commands and boundaries.

Let's get it out in the open: Toddlers are SMART! Babies are SMART! These are little humans that we're talking about. Your child is an eternal being with its own mind, will and emotions.

Baby Houdini

I remember when my family lived in Spokane, WA. I was two years old. I remember so much of that house. I have fond memories of saying goodbye to my dad as he left for work in the mornings, of playing with my favorite walking/meowing stuffed cat and trying to steal my sister's glass pretties off of her dresser. I remember the basic layout of the floor plan, the colors of the carpet, our housekeeper, etc. I was a very active toddler, into everything. I scared the life out of my mother more times than not.

Occasionally, I got out of my crib, went down to the kitchen, and dumped every medicine in the cabinet out onto the floor and counter. I don't really remember that, but my mom shared the story with me time and time again. She was terrified and started locking my door from the outside at night so I would be safe from myself.

Even though I don't remember firsthand what caused me to be locked in my room, I do remember being locked in there. I remember wanting out, and what it was like to no longer have the freedom I craved. I can still picture what my room looked like in the glow of my night light. I had a potty seat, some stuffed animals and a very real thought in my head that if I could find a skinny-enough toy to put through the crack of the door, that I might be able to slide it up high enough to release the latch of the lock. (It was a hook and eye style lock) I was not old enough to communicate these plans, but I had them.

I moved my potty seat against the door to stand on and began my search for something that would work. I thought to myself: What would be long enough, skinny enough and strong enough to release the lock? I failed over and over, but at least I had thought it through.

Although I'm fairly smart today, I'm no genius. My point is this: as soon as your child starts to show any form of willful disobedient behavior, it is time to correct their behavior. That doesn't always mean punish; but more often that means channel. My parents were wise enough to give me toys and other challenges that made use of my budding abilities. A child is raw material looking for applications.

Again, our kids are smart. They know what they are doing. The chaos we experience with fits, screaming and hysterics can be managed with consistent, purposeful parenting (CPP).

Chaos is a sign of inconsistent parenting. We also need to recognize the very real war brewing for your child's soul, a war that is underway right now as you sit and read this. This is not cause for panic; it is cause for enlistment. Are you saved? Walking with God? Great! Now, lead your children in the same.

Oh, and be prepared for resistance. The enemy attacks where the treasure is found. The battle is for the hearts and minds of mankind, and it starts with the youngest among us. It's not enough to fight, however. No one ever achieved much by struggling. They achieved much by winning. Jesus is not in the business of losing. Our end goal is not endurance but victory. We are called to win... for ourselves, for our offspring, for the Kingdom of God on earth as it is in heaven.

Correct your son, and he will give you rest; yes, he will give delight to your soul.

Proverbs 29:17

Two-Way Street

Have you ever had a boss with poor communication skills? What they expected from you was never clear? Perhaps you got reprimanded one day for stepping out too far, and on other days you couldn't step out far enough. As an adult, that type of atmosphere is exhausting to work in. So, why would we ever want that for our children? Yet that is often what occurs in the home as frustrated parents clash with frustrated children. We need to realize that vague boundary lines allow the enemy to come in and destroy our fruit. (think of deer and a garden fence)

Communication is a two-way street. It is important to teach your kids to communicate at all ages.

Little people want to communicate but need to be taught how. How many toddlers do you see screaming disrespectful and willful demands at their parents who frantically hand over crackers, cookies, toys and the like to avoid public embarrassment? How many toddlers do you see getting away with humongous tantrums at restaurants and stores? Parents, if your toddlers are screaming demands at you, allow me to join the fray: *You don't have to endure that!*

Consider the simplicity of meal-time sign language. When my kids were small, around six months old, they weren't much on verbalization. Cavemen had better communication skills. So, I decided to teach my kids to sign for what they wanted. The time and frustration (*a lot* of frustration) in teaching them far outweighed the stress of screaming toddlers in a restaurant surrounded by friends and family. And it was way better than beating the dinner table with their clubs.

As my littles learned to eat, they also learned manners. They learned they didn't get their way with screams and smacking their tray. Throwing their water cups didn't get them a refill. They learned through love, patience, and consistency that they could communicate what they wanted with signing. They were not old enough to talk but they were old enough to show what they wanted through simple signs. They adapted quickly.

DISCIPLINE IN MODERN TIMES

Of course, just because I see parenting issues doesn't mean I am judging the parents or the kids. We all see it, especially when it's happening to us. The difference is in perspectives. We are all in our own battle! I long to support parents walking through these difficulties. This is a rough road, and with all the culturally saturated articles telling us that we will destroy our children, we are uber cautious in discipline. The last thing we want to do is scar our children for life, causing them years of therapy while they dress in black and write songs about hating their parents.

With fear leading the discipline choices of our culture, children and adults alike are struggling more and more with self-harm, depression, and severe anxiety. It's not getting better; it's getting worse.

Teaching your children discipline will shape and mold them *and you* into better human beings. You will learn perseverance, patience, self-control and the success that comes from these Spirit-led qualities. At times, you'll want to throw a fit of your own. You'll want to toss the water cup, bang your spoon against the table, throw yourself down in Wal-Mart kicking and screaming in unknown tongues.

Don't. Take a breath. Be consistent and persistent. Keep trying. It's ok that you want to throw in the towel, but it's not ok to throw in the towel. The fruit is worth your effort! And don't forget who is watching you... every second... of every day. They don't miss a trick.

The fruits of the Spirit are taught from birth. The goal of training your children and teaching obedience is not to rule and control their lives but instead to build their trust that they can discipline themselves.

From the Bible stories we read, we learned that obedience brings life and freedom, but most of these lessons were taught to adults encountering God for the first time. With such a strong instruction manual, however, why wait to teach our kids until they have already gained bad habits? Why would we allow them to disobey and act out as toddlers and not learn something from it? Discipline deferred is opportunity wasted. In the long run, it's a hard road to travel. Just ask Abraham.

IN THE MOMENT

Bringing correction to littles needs to be instant. When correcting and disciplining toddlers, you cannot say things like, "we'll deal with this when we get home." That doesn't work. It matters not whether you'll be home in two hours or ten minutes. With little ones, correction needs to be in the moment, always, even if that means pulling over the car, leaving the theater or the restaurant to take them to a more private location. Do it. Take the time when they're young to show them they mean more to you than your appearance, time or the next scene in the movie. (It's probably just some car chase anyway.)

He who spares the rod hates his son, but he who loves him disciplines him promptly.

Proverbs 13:2

Truly loving our kids means we discipline them promptly, consistently and lovingly. To discipline means *to disciple*—to teach. We don't punish our kids to get our way—that's acting as bad as a ticked-off toddler. Rather, we correct for our children's benefit and ours. In healthy disciplining, we do so with the understanding that our children are different than we are; they need not conform to our ideal box. Proper discipline yields freedom by respecting a child's unique personality.

We should not discipline because we fear the opinions of those around us. We are not to seek our own agenda. Our goal should always be God's agenda. His agenda is to show our children that they belong to Him, that they are loved and that His boundaries of right and wrong are clearly established for health and safety, not control.

Teaching self-control, in particular, is one of the single most important things you will ever do. It is also one of the most time consuming, treacherous, tedious things you will ever do. But if you long to walk in joy and peace and show love to your kids, you will persist.

My son, do not despise the chastening of the Lord, nor detest His correction; For whomever the Lord loves He corrects, just as a father the son in whom he delights.

Proverbs 3:11-12

DISCIPLINE LEADS TO FREEDOM

Freedom—what is freedom? True freedom is getting to do what you want, but only up to the point that it takes away the freedom of another.

The right to swing my fist ends where the other man's nose begins.

Oliver Wendell Holmes

Our kids need to learn this very important part of freedom as young as possible.

Little one, you can do what you like until it interferes with the freedoms of others.

Me

I am an American and a patriot, yet where I live, freedoms are flaunted, abused and often misunderstood. But in my heart, true freedom is cherished; in my family, freedoms are taken seriously.

Your freedom—as a parent, as an adult, as a human being in the likeness of God—is as important as your child's freedom. Parents, we need to stop letting our kids rule our world! Obviously nap routines and potty breaks get priority, but our kids were born to our families. They are members of the collective, not the leaders... not yet. You as the adult, following the leading of the Holy Spirit, get to choose what your child's freedom looks like.

You should be able to shop, go to public events, attend church, watch a movie, visit a friend's house... without feeling miserable, tied down, or having to leave early because your child is a wrecking ball. Good routines, healthy, consistent boundaries, loads of love, patience and prompt discipline create an atmosphere for freedom, peace and joy in parenting.

MY STORIES

Perhaps some stories of how this looked in my life will help you see what I mean. Early in my parenting life, I resolved that my kids' behavior would not dictate my life. I was (and still am) their mother. I'm also an adult with real needs. I need to grocery shop. I need social interactions. I need to shower. I need to sleep! (I need to write this book.)

I praise God for the many moms who went before me and led me in achieving such missions! Having an active life is no easy task when you have littles in tow. With babies, the things that need to be packed just to survive an outing can be overwhelming. We rented a trailer! (joke) But the effort was worth it to me. My kids are a part of my life today because God chose them to be part of my life. He knows my personality, my needs and the fabric of my life.

Yes, life changes when a baby is born, but life doesn't need to stop. Life's outings definitely should not be ruled by the behavior of your children. You can adjust your life to meet their needs, and they can adjust to meet yours.

At the birth of our first baby, I was a Varsity Cheer coach for our local high school. My husband and I were also assistant youth Pastors at our church. As if that wasn't enough, my husband was going to school full-time and working full-time. Our little man, Judea, entered a very busy life of service. We had decided before we had kids that we would raise them in the church. (We were there so much, that is a literal statement). Where we went, he went.

Because I coached cheer, I had practice from 3-5 pm every school day and games two days a week. I brought Judea everywhere with me. He slept attached to me, in my arms, strapped to my belly, in his stroller, wherever he could catch his nap. He was loved by my team, the youth, other staff members, and our church grandmas. It was amazing. I learned to change diapers on my lap. We had so much fun together.

As he grew into a toddler, I toted his walker and toys to practice and youth group. He fell asleep in my arms, on or under the pews of the church, or in the arms of another leader. (Which was amazing because he fought sleep like the Hulk!) He loved being a part of our lives, and we loved him being a part of ours. In all that, he was much like me—busy, strong-willed and short-tempered. He wanted what he wanted, when he wanted it.

I know this sounds simple. In a way it was because I had made up my mind on what we were going to do. I established clear boundaries for him. I found private places for discipline everywhere we went and regularly stopped conversations with: "Excuse me, I will be right back. I need to mom." I took some lessons from my walk with the Lord, understanding that self-control was one of the most important things to teach my children.

As an adult experiencing an array of conflicting pressure, I still battle daily with self-control. But my kids shouldn't have to struggle to the same degree I do. I should win some battles for them, and if I can do that simply by having firm boundaries, yes please!

We've all taken treks to the grocery store with our perfect little angels in tow. For those of us who live in the country, a grocery shopping experience consists of an hour drive to reach a store, then at least three different stores to gather all of the needs of the family (hundred pounds of sugar, yeast and copper line) for a two-week span, though a month is preferable. Successful outings take time, preparation and a lot of patience.

Unfortunately, children don't have a lot of patience.

Now, some would say, "Find a babysitter; it's not worth it." Or "It's too hard on the little ones to go with you."

I will say, as always, that this is a Holy Spirit question. However, my predilection is that they should be with you. Yes, it's hard on everyone, but everyone together is a family unit, growing and learning to contribute. It's not just the grocery store; it's one of the best training grounds for good behavior and hearing the Holy Spirit in moments of chaos... for both parent and child!

Often a single trip for us would look like this.

Before entering the store, I make sure to feed, burp and change my baby. I remind older children A and B of the proper behavior in the store and what is expected as we maneuver the isles.

We enter the store, select a cart and negotiate who gets to sit in the front, who gets to push, and who is along for the ride. I remove the list from my purse, look at the specials on produce, am testing the firmness of the grapefruit when one of the littles announces she has to go pee. Two trips to the bathroom later, we are back on track.

Time flies by. They're tired, I'm tired. We're finishing up in the frozen aisle with a gallon of ice cream when child A remembers something from aisle 1 that they wanted. How will this play out? I manage a firm "No" without receiving a rebellious confrontation. Victory in Jesus!

I get into a long line for checkout, wondering why the store can't hire more people. Finally, it's my turn when child B starts doing the *"I gotta poop and it's coming out now!"* dance. I leave my cart and the melting ice cream, grab my baby and rush child B to the bathroom. Meanwhile, the baby is crying because she's bored—not hungry, just bored and wants my attention. Everyone stares at me as my baby vocalizes her anguish. Eyes of judgment pierce my armor from all sides. *What's wrong with that mother?*

I manage to press through the accusing looks and move on. I know the joy of the Lord is my strength. I was made for such a time as this. Yet *this* is enough to test anyone's nerves. In these moments, prayer is the only thing that keeps me together.

One store down, two to go.

Store number two may lead to screaming tantrums because child A wants a toy from the shelve that is conveniently placed at his level and I say "No." The temptation to give in is real. But I expect it; I'm ready for what might lie ahead. It seems like I've been in this forsaken store for years. He begins to whine longingly and build. I long with all my being for him to simply shut up and us to be back home in comfortable surroundings far from the piercing eyes of the prying public. The whine turns to a loud-ear piercing cry and he begins to stomp his feet.

I want to give him the toy because he's had to go through the dreadful store with me. He's got to be even more exhausted than I am. I wish I had a toy to distract me. I feel sorry for the little fella because it's a lot to handle. What am I going to do? Do I win or does he?

In truth, tiny tot doesn't need a new toy. Tiny tot needs a consistent, loving, firm parent to be strong enough to teach some boundaries. I said "No." I mean "No." He needs to be reminded that he doesn't get his way by throwing a fit, and if tiny tot decides to lose his temper and throw a fit, he will be disciplined (by the consistent, firm, loving, exhausted parent) for crossing the boundary.

Al Davis' famous mantra seems fitting here: *Just win, baby!*

Now, you might be asking yourself: Is it really about winning? YES! It's all about winning. Moments like these are when the foundations are laid. In the grocery store spotlight is when your character is on display for your child to judge.

They listen to you breathe.

They watch how you handle every single step.

They examine your face—red in frustration, pale in exhaustion, pinched in worry.

They wonder: Is she going to act out in her flesh or her Spirit? And equally important: What of theirs are you going to feed?

Every trip you take with your child is a homeschool lesson, a microcosm for life. You are your children's teacher from conception until they carry you away. No one departs parenthood vertically. You will teach your children the foundations of life for the rest of your life, influencing even their grandparenting style. Parenting extends well beyond the grave; it is a living legacy passed on for generations.

This is why something as mundane as a grocery trip involves planning for rest and recreation. While you're in the store, you need to have fun together. You need to bring toys. You need to keep yourself under control. You need to anticipate the irritations that a trip like that will bring. It's a part of parenting. Put on your big girl or big boy pants and don't take those stresses out on your kids. Take your kids to the park to run off some steam between stores, and play *with* them.

These are the days of your life. You should not leave your kids at home out of convenience. I know it's tempting. OK, for an occasional self-treat, do it! But overall, you are on this earth with a major calling—to teach the next generation. This is a serious calling; it should not be taken lightly. Your children should not get shuffled simply because you are stressed out and it's inconvenient. You brought them into this world, now bring them with you.

EXCUSE ME

As harsh as this may seem, I love you enough to tell you the truth—your kids will never be convenient. Ministry opportunities rarely are. You will experience joy and see fruit, and you will have great freedom in your calling, but it takes HARD work to prepare the ground. You must walk in all the fruits of the Spirit. You must choose every day who you will serve: God or self. If you choose self, the fruit will be bitter, delayed or rotten.

Serving yourself can be disguised as serving your children. It's usually found under the guise of "they're tired," "they don't understand" or "it's too much for them to handle." Those are just excuses for "I'm tired and don't want to deal with the war of correcting the behavior I should have corrected years ago because I am at my wit's end and might lose it."

I am not saying it's always that, but we have to be honest with ourselves and admit when we're the tired ones, the cranky ones, or the ones throwing a tantrum (on the inside, of course).

Parents who give in to their children's wants and fits by excusing away their behavior need to understand something. No matter what the underlying reasons, bad behavior is bad behavior. If you need to get to the root of why your child is always tired, that is up to you (and I hope you do), but your child should not be throwing tantrums in the store (or anywhere else), even if they're tired.

We as adults cannot throw tantrums when we're tired. Our children should not be throwing tantrums when they're tired. Our teenagers, ten-year-olds, five-year-olds, four-year-olds, three-year-olds, two-year-olds, and yes, even our one-year-olds should not throw fits. Period. And when they do—I say *when* because even though they shouldn't, they will try and try again—their behavior must be corrected immediately.

Helping your kiddo work through their feelings and gain some self-control through the circumstance is key. Affirming statements can be helpful. "I know you are tired, but you still don't get to act that way." Then if they don't change their behavior, bring discipline, consistently every single time. And for Pete's sake, make sure they get regular rest! (Especially if they're not named *Pete*.)

Discipline begins at home. If you aren't consistent at home, you'll be negotiating with a barbarian when they're tired in public. Behavior change is not something to try in a store after reading this book. This is something you'll have to practice in your own home first. You can have tiny toddlers with self-control, even the ones with spunky personalities, but let me tell you, you will have to lay your life down to achieve it! Just because your child has a spitfire personality doesn't mean you can't teach them to walk in the fruit of the Spirit and to have self-control. It will just take more effort than a tender, gentle personality type. It will take laying down your life in the moment of correction because you won't want to keep going as many times as it will take to win! Spunky spitfires will fight a looooonnnng fight. I know; I had one. Four-hour tests of *"Who's the Leader?"* were the norm. It's exhausting!

The sacrifice you make is to always be a parent first. Ignoring bad behavior because you're not up for the battle is not an effective strategy. You have to decide that you are going to be

God's warrior for your kids every single day, *every moment of every single day*. God will show you which battles to fight! Pray! Sometimes, you have to fight all of the battles! Don't let weariness or exhaustion dictate!

Oh, and don't give in to couch parenting.

couch parenting /kouCH perən(t)iNG/, *noun*: when a parent instructs their child from a couch, and child ignores instruction, then parent gets louder and threatens action but doesn't actually get up from said couch to address behavior in question.

I remember having to lay my nursing baby down, milk spraying everywhere, because one of my kids decided to disobey me. She figured I wouldn't come after her because I was nursing. She was wrong. With the baby gasping for more, I had to take that moment to show my child that boundaries are boundaries, and yes, I will enforce them. It's not a fight for territory. Rather, it's a demonstration of how much that child means to me. Teaching her was worth the interruption.

We cannot couch parent, period. And we should not use our older children as proxy parents. Of course, I am guilty of all of that. (How do you think I learned not to do it?) No one is perfect. The point is to recognize what we are doing and change to the right behavior. Lazy parenting does not produce good fruit. Couch parenting demonstrates that our fatigue decides our boundaries, and having our older children parent provokes bitterness between siblings and parents.

Parenting is the most difficult job on the planet. It never stops; however, rest is attainable if we choose to do what's right even when we're exhausted. If we consistently follow through, keep our promises, letting our *yes* mean *yes* and our *no* mean *no*, (ref. Matthew 5:37), then when we are exhausted, our children will trust us at our word and obey without a fight. (And you might not have to leave the couch after all!)

True boundaries build a foundation of trust and are easier in the long run.

As you persevere in parenting, I can guarantee two things:

1. Your kids will embarrass you
2. You will feel like you're beating your head against a brick wall.

5
In Jesus We Build

ONE OF THE MOST IMPORTANT THINGS God has taught me in the area of discipline is to not be offended. As strange as this may sound, it is far too easy to fall into offense with our children over their particularly egregious behavior because, as their parents, we are emotionally involved. However, our kids will also be our brothers and sisters in Christ someday (way before you're ready for it), so we need to address them as such in the area of offense.

God was serious when he taught me this lesson. Offense will fog our vision and cloud our judgment. There are many scriptures dealing with offense, but Matthew 18:15 is the first that comes to mind.

> *Moreover, if your brother sins against you, go and tell him his fault between you and him alone. If he hears you, you have gained your brother...*
>
> Matthew 18:15

When your child sins against you, go to him in private. Love him enough to do so.

> *And above all things have fervent love for one another, for love covers a multitude of sins.*
>
> 1 Peter 4:8

Approach is everything. If you are in public or in front of other siblings, speak quietly and directly to your child so as not to uncover or expose them. And if speaking quietly will still be heard by those near, then go to somewhere private. If you do what needs to be done to correct the behavior and yet it continues, readdress the issue and be consistent. If you are married, you can always get your spouse involved, but correct in unity! (Remember: divide and conquer is the enemy's potent strategy.)

If you and your spouse have worked on the behavior consistently at home and it's still a problem, or if you are a single parent in need of some assistance, ask your spiritual leadership. God created a generational church on purpose. Youth bring life and zeal; elders bring grounding and wisdom. However, always let the Holy Spirit into your decision making.

We all want perfect kids. We don't want to be embarrassed and we never want it to be our kid when we hear over the grocery store intercom: "Tantrum on aisle four. *Tantrum* on aisle four. Cleanup crew respond."

Let's be real, however. It will happen to you someday, if it hasn't happened multiple times already. The key is to expect it and be prepared to teach when the opportunity presents itself. If you do that, temper fits will be a rare occurrence!

If, however, you allow your energy to be diverted to fueling an offense toward the offending child, how will you see clearly to teach and discipline? If you are worried about what others think about you, you will discipline under the fear of man, and your focus will be there and not on what the Holy Spirit is trying to speak to you in that very critical moment.

Prepare your heart. Be willing to be interrupted constantly, especially when they're little. Be ready for surprises—pleasant and aggravating. Know that if you close yourself off to one experience, you'll miss all the other experiences. The little people around us are not perfect—they're humans, just like everyone else. Effective parenting starts with knowing who they are.

Kids can be aggravating, especially when they have something on their minds. Babies are born knowing instinctively how to get your attention—they have to survive. But when older children try to break into your conversation with another adult, it can be tempting to forcibly ignore them, hence the adage of "Children should be seen and not heard." (Which I strongly disagree with, mind you)

The key, however, is not that outdated excuse for youthful repression, but to teach your children to interrupt adult conversations politely. This technique is something I gleaned from an amazing, older mom who took me under her wing. She taught her children to put their hand on her and wait quietly until she addressed them. This might seem like a small thing, but it has been such a gift to both my children and me. In teaching it to my children, I took the time to explain that this simple act helps me respectfully give them my full attention when they speak while still respecting the other people in the room. I longed to hear what they had to say, but if they burst into the room without restraint, I'd miss what the other person was saying to me, which is disrespectful to all involved.

HAND TO THE PLOW

Training your children will be inconvenient. It will be hard. It will be exhausting. So be it. When is plowing a field easy? It's sweaty, grueling work. Planting a field in the right season takes sacrifice. Floods will come, heat will come, pestilence and drought are sureties. Yet perseverance is the key to desired results.

Consistent discipline leads to walking in the Spirit and not giving way to the flesh. It teaches self-control and shows a clear boundary of what you expect. If you set that boundary and follow through time and time again, family outings will be a joy. It works for you, the parent, and it works for your kids. They will be thankful to know what to expect, and in turn, you will feel like giving them gifts out of love and joy and not desperation. You won't be racked with the guilt of feeling that you lost the battle, the war and the kingdom.

> *Therefore, brethren, we are debtors—not to the flesh, to live according to the flesh. For if you live according to the flesh you will die; but if by the Spirit you put to death the deeds of the body, you will live. For as many as are led by the Spirit of God, these are sons of God, for you did not receive the spirit of bondage again to fear, but you received the Spirit of adoption by, whom we cry, "Abba, Father." The Spirit Himself bears witness with our spirit that we are children of God, and if children, then heirs—heirs of God and joint heirs with Christ, if indeed we suffer with Him, that we may also be glorified together.*
>
> Romans 8:12-17

Teach your kids to live in the fruit of the spirit and they will naturally eschew the fruit of the flesh. The sooner, the better. The flesh only gets more difficult to correct the longer it grows. What you feed will grow.

As children grow, the form of discipline you use should evolve with them. A good rule of thumb with toddler behavior (even though it can be unbelievably adorable) is that if you do not want them acting that way at 15 years, they should not get away with it at 15 months. Your 15-month-old should not throw things, hit you, hit their nursery mates, steal toys, shout "No" at you, etc. These behaviors need immediate correcting, every single time! And remember: correction does not always have to include punishment. Listen to the Holy Spirit. Sometimes, redirecting them and praising their new behavior is sufficient.

Now, if you already have a 15-year-old and you've missed your opportunity to lay these boundaries in the younger years, don't fret. Your life with them is not over. It is going to take a lot more patience, consistency, love, faithfulness and genuine character on your part than it would have when they were little, but it is doable.

It's not over until it's over.

And it's never over.

As my son, Judea, entered his tween years (ages 9 – 12), the Lord revealed this beautiful thing He does for our children. He gave me a vision of Judea with aviator style, rose-colored goggles. Then he spoke to me and said:

This is what I've done for you up until this point. You have been viewed through rose-colored goggles. Everything you did was lovely, true and covered in grace in his little eyes. You were an amazing supermom. Now, I will remove those goggles so that he can see you all the way. Your character flaws will be revealed. The blemishes in how you live will no longer be covered by my grace goggles. He will see you clearly.

Be mindful—he will look carefully as he watches your every move. He will watch how you deal with disappointment, failure, fear and success. I allow this so that he can decide what kind of man he wants to be. As he moves into the age of accountability, he will judge many, not because he longs to be judgmental but because he longs to know what being a man of God looks like.

This marks the time in a preteen's life when authenticity and truth are the most critical. Our tweeny teens are looking. They are begging for boundaries, for something authentic, and all we can offer is Jesus. Fundamentally, this is no different than the toddler years. Discipline is still a huge factor, but it's the application that is different.

In a perfect world, a tween's identity is already found solidly in Christ, but the enemy is at work and wants to destroy their identity with everything he can. Unfortunately, if you are not aware, if you are not consistently parenting with purpose (CPP), your words can be used as the enemy's weapons from birth to the time you die. Your words and actions can be a most destructive tool.

> *Death and life are in the power of the tongue,*
> *and those who love it will eat its fruits.*
>
> Proverbs 18:21

With our mouths we bring blessing and cursing. The power of life and death is in the tongue.

When our children hit their tween years and those rose-colored goggles come off, what are they going to see and hear? Will you be the reason they flourish? Or the reason they stumble?

I have been both for my kids. I am thankful that God got ahold of me and spoke truth into my spirit. But for many years I lived under the fear of man, succumbing to the lie that I wasn't good enough, deceived that it was solely up to me to make my kids into something.

You will know the truth, and the truth will set you free.

John 8:32 ESV

The truth... Yes, I am responsible for my children. I do have to work hard to diligently teach them, but it is not up to me to do anything but obey the Holy Spirit. Jesus is the only one who can make our hearts soft. He will lead me and guide me. I do not have to come up with the ways to parent. I do not have to do anything more than what He asks of me. Where I am weak, He is strong.

Being a parent is naturally exhausting work. You will be tired, but it is rewarding. Don't hide behind the lies that the enemy tries to spoon feed you that the misbehavior of a wee one is ok. Don't be lazy and stay on the couch when they yell at you with disrespect. I know it's cute when they're 2, but it's annoying at 12, abhorrent at 22, and when they're 42, they'll be stealing your social security checks.

The law of sowing and reaping is very real.

Do not be deceived, God is not mocked [He will not allow Himself to be ridiculed, nor treated with contempt nor allow His precepts to be scornfully set aside]; for whatever a man sows, this <u>and this only</u> is what he will reap.

Galatians 6:7 Amp

We need to sow all the seeds of the fruit to reap the harvest. Depending on when you acquire this truth, your kids may not yet be ready to receive seed. The thorns and lies might be too thick. Perhaps some weeding will need to be done before the ground can even be prepared. But the ground's past doesn't determine its future. You do, the Lord does. With hard work, diligence and dedication your child's foundation can still be laid, even if you think the house is half up—a bit off kilter, but standing.

TEENS, FOSTER, OR NEWLY ADOPTED-IT'S NEVER TOO LATE

He put another parable before them, saying, "The kingdom of heaven may be compared to a man who sowed good seed in his field, but while his men were sleeping, his enemy came and sowed weeds among the wheat and went away. So when the plants came up and bore grain, then the weeds appeared also. And the servants of the master of the house came and said to him, 'Master, did you not sow good seed in your field? How then does it have weeds?' He said to them, 'An enemy has done this.' So the servants said to him, 'Then do you want us to go and gather them?' But he said, 'No, lest in gathering the weeds you root up the wheat along with them. Let both grow together until the harvest, and at harvest time I will tell the reapers, "Gather the weeds first and bind them in bundles to be burned, but gather the wheat into my barn."'"

Matthew 13:24-30

Consider this lesson as applying to the effort to straighten out a wayward teen. At this point, the good wheat is growing with the bad wheat and there is no way to differentiate until both come to fruition. Trying to weed out all the wrong in a teen will destroy the good in them. At some point in a child's life, it's too late to weed. You will have to let the wheat you planted grow among weeds. It's a critical time in their life for receiving identity. Don't cause more damage. Pray and obey! The Holy Spirit will lead and guide you in how to guide them. Remember, only the Lord can soften hearts! Trying to correct every wrong in a foster child, a newly adopted child, or a teen, even one who has lived with godly leadership their entire life, is counterproductive. These are times to lean in hard to the Lord, pray fervently for wisdom and truth, and receive copious quantities of mercy and grace. God will lead.

He will show you what to pull, when to pull, and what to leave. Fruit is still an option. It's all in His hands.

DON'T FORCE YOUR KIDS TO WORSHIP

While it is possible to force a child into just about any behavior, the results will be external, not internal. In fact, the work on the inside will be in opposition to everything being inflicted on them from without. This is disastrous.

God is the only one who can soften our hearts. We need to remember His promises. In Proverbs 22:6 it says, "Train up a child in the way they should go, and when they are old they will not depart from it." We have to trust God with our diligent work, even if it's just beginning. As we trust Him and do our best, His grace will cover the rest.

We are flawed. I hate it but it's true. I am going to fall short, and I am the first to tell my children that! I tell my children all the time that as parents, we are going to screw things up! We don't always pray first. We don't always listen to the Lord. We don't always respond in the fruit of the Spirit.

As adults, we need to be first to repent and admit when we are wrong. We need to diligently reach for Jesus and submit to growth ourselves! Be an obedient child yourself and everything else will follow. I cannot make my teenager believe what I believe. *I can't.* I can't force him into the Kingdom. Remember Sarai? How did control work for her? Instead, I can war in the Spirit. I can live in obedience and walk in peace and truth myself. In doing so, I naturally show how good God is. Our teens don't need convincing or forcing. They need to be influenced by our genuine humility and truth of life. The hard things are hard, but doable in Christ. Show it by the way you live day to day.

Just as forcing your kids to worship is futile, compelling them to read the Bible is not always the answer either. In our home, we had our kids learn scripture when they were little. We made it as fun as possible with rewards, etc. I did make my kids read books during homeschool time that were not their favorites, but they helped lay a foundation of knowledge. Yet as teens, making them read God's Word when they don't want to will bring negative fruit. It will be read with bitterness and anger... if they read it at all. What good will that accomplish? Why force it? Does God force me to do things? Does He guilt-trip me into things? No, He doesn't. He knows better. So should we.

As parents, we require our children to show respect in church. This includes staying off their phone (other than taking notes or reading scripture), standing during worship, etc. We have taken the time to teach our children that this is not forced worship but demanded respect for those around them and the God that we, the parents, choose to serve. They are not required to spend time with the Lord, but they are highly encouraged to do so. Travis and I practice Deuteronomy 6 as much as possible!

Here are the first four verses of this sacred text:

Now this is the commandment—the statutes and the rule—that the Lord your God commanded me to teach you, that you may do them in the land to which you are going over, to possess it, that you may fear the Lord your God, you and your son and your son's son, by keeping all his statutes and his commandments, which I command you, all the days of your life, and that your days may be long. Hear therefore, O Israel, and be careful to do them, that it may go well with you, and that you may multiply greatly, as the Lord, the God of your fathers, has promised you, in a land flowing with milk and honey.

Deuteronomy 6:1-4 ESV

Travis and I are blessed that our kids choose to worship. They engage because they've seen the fruit in our lives and their friends' lives. They've heard testimony after testimony. They've gained some of their own testimonies. Leading a child in their walk with the Lord should be not fear-driven nor religious. Indeed, it can't be! I can encourage them and talk to them about being ready for battle, etc., but I can't force it. I have to listen to the Holy Spirit when encouraging because often, in fear, I want to control them! I want their preparation for battle to look like mine. I want to keep them from all pain. However, I need to understand that my kids are going to get hurt. They're going to get a few wounds along the way. As long as I protect them from the fatal ones, that's how they learn. Yes, there are times to step in! I am not saying stand back and watch them get owned by the culture and the enemy! But there are also times to step back, especially as they grow into themselves. The key is to seek the Lord, be wise and don't be led by fear!

Mr. Rogers said it best: We need to remember what it was like to be their age!

- Remember the peer pressure?
- Remember the insecurities?
- Remember the fear and self-doubt?
- Remember the hard things you faced?
- Remember the hormones?
- Remember the things that consumed your thoughts and drove your decisions?

Try to remember! Being a kid is HARD! Connecting with your teens can be equally HARD! One of the biggest reasons is because adults refuse to remember what it was like. Kids don't think we even remotely understand what they're going through, and to a degree, we don't! We don't because life today is different than it was when we were young! The reality is that our children face things we didn't have to. Be open and flexible to the Lord, allowing Him to completely change your mind on how to handle a situation. Listen to your children! *Listen...!*

When your kids are little, they take a ton of your time and energy. You have to parent on purpose, get off the couch a million times, cook all of their meals, wash all of their clothes, do all the chores yourself, even do their bathroom maintenance. You do everything.

When your kids are older, however, the time commitment is the same but it looks different. Now, they can do chores, make their own lunches, and help with the day to day, but their emotions and hormones are all over the place. Their identity is under brutal attack, and they are in search of who they are. Their world is in upheaval as it offers a myriad of false solutions to real or contrived dilemmas.

As a parent, you need to be stable, consistent and above all: *honest!* You don't have to handle every situation perfectly and without flaw or hiccough, but in genuine surrender to the Lord. Your teen still needs clear boundaries, discipline and unconditional love. They also need you to speak life and truth more than ever before. The time you used to spend rocking and snuggling them, you will now spend driving them to sports practice or music lessons or sitting in silence watching them play a video game. You will be listening into the night about the day's hardships while praying for the daily war at hand. The details shift. The effort remains the same.

If I can tell you anything to do for your teen, it's to invest your time... to listen, to pray, to advise, to withhold advice, to speak, to remain silent. Do not take your new freedom from the physical needs as freedom to do whatever you want. Sometimes you just need to shut up and sit in the same room with your teens: no demands, no corrections, no instructions, just time-sharing space. Open your ears; open your heart. Pray as they speak and definitely pray before you speak! Teens are not going to see eye to eye with you. That's natural. You're going to disagree, sometimes about big things. Don't panic! This is called *normal.* It's healthy, even necessary.

Trust the Lord. Breathe! Shut up. Listen. Ask the Holy Spirit. And advise with wisdom.

Remember, you are a parent until you die. It will vary in waves, at times easier and then harder. It's that way because you love deeply and want the best. You see things they can't see, but can't control the outcome all the time. It's hard! But it's going to be OK! Discipline still needs to happen when your kids are teens. I like to call teenager-hood the *toddler-round two.* The manipulation tactics and struggle for independence are the same. Of course, the harder work you do when they are toddlers, the easier are the teen years. Yes, this is when the rise of flesh begins, and with it the toe-to-toe battles, but if you have been consistent and purposeful in parenting, your kids know that you will keep your word and that it's not worth it to oppose you. They'll know you are fighting *for* them and not *against* them because you demonstrate it on a daily basis.

This is why my favorite thing to do when things get heated with older kids is to have them go to their room. It gives me time to pray and get over my offense to see clearly through God's lens. And who knows... God may be waiting for them on the other side of their door.

SUMMARY

Maybe this chapter has been a bit of a discipline for you? Maybe this was a nudge to get you onto the path the Lord wants you on? The Lord has spoken these things to me time and time again, often as correction. The Lord regularly uses his rod and staff on this wandering sheep to keep her on the right path.

Here are some scriptures on being a son and being disciplined by the Lord and by an earthly father. Discipline is a key tool God uses to show sonship. We feel safe and loved when we know what is expected and when it's upheld. Hearing God, consistency and love are key.

And you have forgotten the exhortation which speaks to you as to sons:

My son, do not despise the chastening of the Lord, nor be discouraged when you are rebuked by Him; For whom the Lord loves He chastens, and scourges every son whom He receives."

IF you endure chastening, God deals with you as sons: for what son is there whom a father does not chasten? But if you are without chastening, of which all have become partakers, then you are illegitimate and not sons. Furthermore, we have had human fathers who corrected us, and we paid them respect. Shall we not much more readily be in subjection to the Father of spirits and live? For they indeed for a few days chastened us as seemed best to them, but He for our profit, that we may be partakers of His holiness. Now no chastening seems to be joyful for the present, but painful; nevertheless, afterward it yields the peaceable fruit of righteousness to those who have been trained by it."

Hebrews 12:5-11 NKJV

CHAPTER DISCUSSION QUESTIONS

1. In what ways are your kids stealing your freedom?
2. How is that affecting your peace and joy?
3. Do you feel free to grocery shop, visit with friends, and family, and go to restaurants with your kids and overall experience peace?
4. Are there any areas you see where your boundaries have not been made clear or consistently enforced?
5. Are you guilty of couch parenting, or having older children parent for you?
6. Do you discipline promptly, or have you been in the habit to let things slide until the behavior builds to the point that you nearly implode?
7. Are you guilty in fear-based correction?
8. Are you being honest in your sin and shortcomings with the Lord, repenting and heeding His correction?

6

Weeding and Warring

OUR CHILDREN ARE GROWING. Someday they'll venture into this world as young men and women of God. We all hope our children will do so with great confidence of who they are in Christ, ready to fulfill His destiny for them. But we live in a world of confusion, a desperate culture grasping for something genuine—a true identity, a meaningful legacy. For our children to not be swept away in the futile search for real values, we need to prepare them and war for them. The sooner we go to battle, the better. We need to take ground! We need to teach them who they are as sons and daughters of the Lord. We need to prepare them to be strong members of society, steadfast husbands and wives, stalwart brothers and sisters.

Raising confident kids secure in who they are is a bloody war. I am in the midst of it now as I write this. I think of my children: ages 15, 13, and 10 years old (as of this writing). They have modern American culture attacking with fierce weapons from every side. The thing is, I have decided to war next to my children. It is amazing, effective and so unbelievably hard.

I imagine my hair frazzled, tangled and askew in the wind. I'm exhausted and yet full of fire, ready for the fight of my life. I have prepared. I have my sword in my hand, my shield at our forefront. My children stand behind me with their swords, ready for war. We are fighting, slaying and shouting as the enemies fall around us in a bloody heap. While I fight, I take the time to talk my kids through the warfare, coaching them as we take another enemy down. I see it now; their little shields of faith growing with every victory. I arm them with the knowledge I already have. I anticipate the enemy's next move, and after I take one down, I talk them through taking down a few on their own. I show them who we're fighting against, what weapons to use, and how to prevail.

> *For we do not wrestle against flesh and blood, but against principalities, against powers, against the rulers of the darkness of this world, against spiritual wickedness in high places.*
>
> Ephesians 6:12 KJV

We don't war against people but against Satan and his forces. He seeks to destroy self-worth through internal hatred and shame. He shines a light on faults too, but instead of healing, he magnifies our sin and makes it normal in our minds. Everyone knows shame when we do something wrong. That happens because deep down we know it's wrong. We know in ourselves when we fall short. Yet the enemy wants to exploit it. Fortunately, Jesus wants to heal us from shame, remove the desire we have to do wrong, give us tools to be forever changed and set us free.

> *Godly sorrow brings repentance that leads to salvation and leaves no regret, but worldly sorrow brings death.*
>
> II Corinthians 7:10

THEREIN LIES THE LIE

Satan wants us to believe we cannot change and that being bound by sin is just the way it is. With our own thought processes, he doesn't have to work very hard. With one whisper, we're led to wallow in shame without Jesus, causing us to self-preserve and cope with weapons that are temporal. The pain hides our underlying conditions. It eats away at self-worth. We grasp for an identity, a legacy, something beautiful and strong even if it's built on sand. If we don't recognize the battle for what it is, we grow sicker and sicker. The lie speaks ever so softly: *This is how it will always be. There is no hope for change. This is who you are. Deal with it.*

Death seeps into our souls, decaying our true identity and slowly moving us further and further from truth. The death-bearing lie takes root. As it grows, infection breeds anxiety, depression and spiritual corruption. We become unbalanced to the depths of our beings, even our cellular structure and chemical responses are changed.

It all starts with a whisper:

> *You will never be enough.*
> *You will never do it right.*
> *You are not honorable*
> *You don't deserve respect.*
> *You will always fail.*
> *Your personality will never fit in.*
>
> The Devil

Whispers can come during or after horribly traumatic situations. Certainly, I am not trying to lessen those. However bad things happen to all of us, and really bad things happen to a few of us. We can't always control what happens, but we can choose how we view ourselves, who we believe, and what we hold responsible for our trauma. We are always accountable, however, for the voice we tune into. The enemy is always whispering, and with that lie, a feeling is stirred that brews offense. If we're not diligent, it then scabs over with bitterness, sealing in the infection and preventing healing.

REELING FROM FEELINGS

There is a lot to be said about feelings. I feel a lot! I am an emotional, passionate person. Because of this, I constantly lean in to Jesus to check myself. I'm talking "praying-without-ceasing" checking. I realize just because I feel something doesn't make it true. I know that I can come and stand under the spotlight of Jesus, and instead of shame and guilt, I'll feel His love and warmth. He baths me in light that protects me. It's a force field keeping darkness at bay. I used to be scared of it. I used to be ashamed of what God would see, but now I rejoice in it. I know it for what it is! I step up, the light shines down, and in that moment, I receive indescribable peace. He reveals all the deception the enemy has planted. Instead of shame and inadequacy, I am overjoyed that I don't have to see everything, He does. As I regularly come, He gently reveals, removes, washes and heals.

In John Bevere's book, *Breaking Intimidation*, he shares a vision of demons that stand upon their surfboards waiting, itching, for someone to speak. And when the words are loosed, the demons surf along the sound waves, twisting the message and bringing lies and sowing discord.

Evil surfs on nonverbal communications as well. A look, a gesture or a certain body posture at an opportune time can be a brutal weapon of the enemy, and he is ever ready to point them out in spades.

Twisting communication is a weapon that stirs feelings toward others, causing us to feel they have a negative attitude about us. These quiet whispers make other's opinions vital to our self-image. Suddenly, with no apparent reason, we feel slighted, insulted, even despised, and we want to strike back. What we forget in those moments of attack is that the enemy sows lies and what he is whispering has nothing to do with the other person's true feelings. The whisper is a projection of our own insecurity.

We need to teach our children to not assume the feelings of others, but to communicate by asking questions. We need to inform them that whispering lies and sowing discord are major tools the enemy uses to destroy relationships. We as adults need to model this, to be humble and ask questions of ourselves. We need to be willing to "Matthew 18" relational problems. (Go to one another instead of assuming we already know everything.)

A lack of true identity can lead to feelings and offenses that bring lies to reality through insecurity and shame. If we're not willing to humble ourselves and talk to the person, before we know it, we're in a muddy lake full of misunderstandings and jagged relationships. How we walk out relationships with our friends, pastors, bosses, coworkers and leaders speaks loudly to our children about integrity and identity.

Remember, they're watching everything we do.

NEW EYES TO SEE THE DAWN

Our children are overwhelmed with feelings. They have no idea where they belong in this world, what they're going to be when they grow up, or to whom they belong unless we show them. We need to! We are responsible to teach them and love them enough to reveal their true identity as belonging to Jesus.

Jesus washes away all insecurity and doubt. Being His removes the fear of man and the need to please others for a place to be ourselves. This is because our place is firmly known.

This starts when our children are little. I will never forget when God spoke to me about my kid's clothing choices. My daughter, Eden, was finally at the age she wanted to dress herself, and she put together the craziest outfits. She would put on patterned leggings with a different patterned skirt. She would often wear two shirts of different patterns and a bright colored jacket and shoes that made the whole thing worse. I'd giggled when I saw her but she beamed with excitement. She LOVED her style! One Sunday, getting ready for church, she came into the room sporting one of her wackiest ensembles. I started to tell her to go change when the Holy Spirit stopped me.

"What are you doing, Mo?" He said with such love.

"I am going to make her change; she looks hilarious."

"She loves what she has on. This is who I made her to be. Look at her!"

I paused and looked at my daughter. I absorbed her—her fun, her silliness, her poise. She was adorable.

As I looked, He spoke again.

"She's comfortable in her own skin. She doesn't care what anyone thinks about her. She is confident in what she likes. Why would you take that away from her and teach her to be insecure and focus on man's opinion when I made her like this?"

I stared at my little girl through fresh tears. She was running and hopping, expressive and excited about the day. I was embarrassed that I almost took that from her. I almost instilled an idea that man's opinion mattered more than God's opinion of her. I almost told her that she looked ridiculous and should change. I almost put her in my box.

At that moment, I realized that I did that with my oldest, Judea. I told him he should have his hair a certain way, wear what I thought were the hippest clothes, told him that he should look cool. Today, I regret it. It caused him so many battles with insecurity, battles I invited, the fruit of seeds I planted unknowingly.

Since that day that Eden graced the living room with radiant joy, I've been careful to speak life into my children to be who God made them, encouraging their individuality to join their identity with the Lord, just as the Holy Spirit spoke to me that Sunday morning.

When they ask "Mom, does this look ok?" I respond with simple truth but not necessarily my opinion. After all, they do look adorable even if their clothes are laughable by my standards. Let's face it: my style is not going to be theirs. I am getting "old."

A Dressing the Issue

We all know that how we dress—the adornment of the body—can be Satan's playground. The world presses in to our children, attempting to sexualize our young daughters and sons. Clothing choices for our children, therefore, can be more than what to wear. We have to care for our children's hearts and teach them to fight for their true identity so that clothing represents them as a son or daughter.

The only way to do that is to address the heart, which we cannot judge nor soften, nor form, but we can war for!

Above all else, guard your heart, for everything you do flows from it.

Proverbs 4:23

We need to teach our children the importance of guarding their hearts with every opportunity that presents itself. We as parents need to war in the Spirit behind closed doors, in the quiet when we're alone with the Lord. We need to fiercely go to battle for them!

For in our children's minds it often comes down to who or what is influencing them, and again, lost ground starts with a whisper: "Everyone else is doing it!" *Everyone*... in school, on TV, in the movies... you know, *everyone*.

Uh huh.

Practically speaking, here is how I handle the clothing issue. I have three rules:

1. Clothing must be weather appropriate.//
2. Clothing must be modest.//
3. Good hygiene must be followed: clean clothing, regular bathing, brushing their teeth and hair, etc.

Appropriate clothing means more than what you reveal. Modesty can be situational. In some circumstances, more skin is appropriate. The beach, the gym...you follow? (I learned this from Lisa Bevere's *Kissed the Girls and Made them Cry*.) It also includes not wearing a superman costume to a wedding or a swimsuit to the grocery store without a cover. I explain to my budding fashion icons that a wedding is a special occasion and we need not take away from the bride and groom on their day. We don't want to be a distraction with our crazy regalia. We are there to share in their celebration, not hijack it.

I admit, some days I still struggle with letting them wear their own styles. At times, I really dislike what my kids pick out. As of this writing, my youngest daughter, Selah, is sporting a single pigtail with her bangs pinned to the opposite side and all of her other hair down. She does this herself so she has some bumps and funky hairs going everywhere. On the inside I'm screaming. I want so badly to fix it, to suggest something "cuter," but she feels so cool and truly loves her hair. And you know what? She rocks it! In that moment I have to remember that as long as their outfits meet my three rules, I have to let it go.

Not every parent appreciates the allowances I make. I've actually had other parents tease my kids' clothing, and in that moment, *Mama Bear is ready to shred their faces.* I guard my children's hearts fiercely, yet I do my best to lead with love and kindness. And in fairness, the teasers don't realize the damage they could cause... which is why their faces remain unscathed.

So, let your kids be themselves within healthy boundaries, and don't tease other people's kids. Instead, encourage them to be who God made them to be and accept their wackadoodle outfits!

SINS OF THE PARENTS

The Lord showed me that we as parents often teach insecurity; we breed it and feed it. It comes out of our own longing for our family to appear *just right*. We like a certain style, we want our family to be picture-perfect, and we *know* what would look best. Yet in the next moment, we talk about how "we don't need to keep up with the Joneses," and that looks aren't everything. We teach our kids not to judge a book by its cover; meanwhile we are decorating our own covers with concern of how we will be judged, and they see it! As a teen, I did a lot of babysitting. One family in particular grew to "adopt" me as one of their own. Although I deeply treasure them and all they did for me, I remember the dad was always pointing out how different people looked stupid to him. He would say things like "Look at them, look how stupid they look! We don't want to look dumb like that, do we kids?"

Weeding and Warring

His children, young and eager to please their dad, would laugh and shout back, "No way!" But the look on their faces told me more. I saw questions in their eyes. They wondered what was wrong with the way those people looked and why they were stupid.

> *And he [Jesus] said: "Truly I tell you, unless you change and become like little children, you will never enter the kingdom of heaven.*
>
> Matt. 18:3

The Lord said we're to be like children to enter the Kingdom of God. I wonder if God had this childlike way of thinking in mind when He wrote this verse. Sometimes, we just need to see things (including ourselves) through the eyes of a child.

Once in a while I struggle with my own self-image and I have to be conscious of what I believe and say about myself in front of my kids. For example, recently I've been feeling old. I don't want to look old yet. I don't want to be outdated. I love fashion and cute clothes. In my moments of insecurity, however, I have to be careful with my words. I am guilty of letting things slip, and the things I say in my struggle have an "other people's approval" tone to them. I regularly self-evaluate why I dress the way I do, wear make-up, etc. I feel confident most of the time; it's when I don't feel confident that I need to be most alert. I wear make-up because it's fun. I enjoy being put together, but I have gone out without it and felt fine. I think that's important for my kids to see. Sometimes I struggle, I feel awkward, insecure and stupid, but God reminds me of who I am. Sometimes, when I stumble, my children remind me to keep my words pure and aligned with what God says about me.

When Travis and I were youth pastors, we were broke... dirt poor. We were trying our hand at owning a paint store and ended up learning a lot. Unfortunately, the price of those lessons cost us more than the business could produce. During that time, I was a stay-at-home mom but still a licensed cosmetologist, so I really cared about my appearance. Due to our poverty, however, I was worried that the youth wouldn't accept me. I didn't own any nice clothes at the time. I had one pair of beat up nurse-style shoes, some ripped jeans (when they weren't in fashion), and company logo t-shirts that we got free from our failing paint store.

The Lord assured me that He is what matters most. He reminded me of John the Baptist who went before Jesus crying "Repent, for the Kingdom of heaven has come near," yet he was clothed in camel hair and lived on locust and wild honey. *Camel hair? In the desert? Didn't that itch?* Yet look at all that he accomplished. He prepared the way of the Lord.

We can get so caught up in being accepted that we forget the authority that lives within us.

Today I teach my kids (and remind myself) that appearance means little, it should be fun, not a mandate to fit in. At best, it is a tool to reach certain types of people. The world does look on outward appearance, but if we are who God made us to be, don't you think we'll reach those who He wants us to reach?

While my struggle was in clothes and makeup, many people struggle with an unhealthy body image. God actually asked a friend of mine if she would be willing to be fat for Him. She was obsessed with health. To reset her thinking, God had her relax her focus on working out and micro-managing her diet for a season so she could rest in being His.

It sounds like an odd question for the Lord to ask: "Would you be fat for me?" but is it? He didn't actually want her to become overweight; He wanted her to be comfortable in Him while being imperfect. Her health-obsessed mindset was unhealthy. She was controlling her life out of desperation due to uncontrollable circumstances and not trusting in God to sustain her. So, she focused on something she thought was good. It became an idol. God asked that question to get her attention.

Are you so obsessed with your own ideas of what things should look like that you've forgotten to ask God what He wants for you or your children?

Pray and ask God what is right for your family. You know if you're eating well and exercising. *You know.* We are either healthy or not. Health is good stewardship of the only body God gave us. That should be the goal, not a number on a scale or a certain body shape. Pursuing all the right curves, super-cut muscles, the latest styles, your house looking like a showroom can be fun things but they should not become platforms for self-mutilation, inflated ego or empty pride.

How do we instill identity in our children when we struggle with our own? The answer is: we live vulnerably. My kids see my shortcomings more than anyone. Allowing God's truth to set us free is essential to keeping them free. We have the keys to the kingdom because we have Jesus. He is our life-source.

Communication is critical. We need to speak openly about the things of this world as our kids face them. We need to give our kids the truth about their hopes and dreams and futures. We need to tell them daily that just because we feel something, doesn't make it true or right or even important. We have to be willing to do the right thing no matter how we feel. Doing the right thing is called *righteousness.*

> *Little children, make sure no one deceives you; the one who practices righteousness is righteous, just as He is righteous.*
>
> 1 John 3:7
>
> *For the Lord is righteous, He loves righteousness; The upright will behold His face.*
>
> Psalm 11:7
>
> *The righteous cry, and the Lord hears and delivers them out of all their troubles.*
>
> Psalm 34:17
>
> *Many are the afflictions of the righteous, But the Lord delivers him out of them all.*
>
> Psalm 34:19
>
> *For the arms of the wicked will be broken, But the Lord sustains the righteous.*
>
> Psalm 37:17
>
> *The righteous will inherit the land and dwell in it forever.*
>
> Psalm 37:29

FALSE FEELINGS

I want to take a moment to consider how quickly we can get off course. Back when my husband, Travis, and I were first married, I misread his facial expressions all the time. You see, Travis is an amazing, patient man with angry-looking eyebrows. I always think of the movie *Toy Story* and packing his "angry eyes," except for him I'd have to pack kind eyes. It's not his fault God gave him stern, beautiful eyes.

Early on, I was not used to his eyes. I regularly assumed he was mad at me. I was also adept at believing that he wanted me to be like his mom. I was certain that he wanted me to keep our home a certain way and have a picture-perfect dinner on the table when he got home from work. Because these are impossible ideals (especially after kids), I was certain I failed him every day because the roast beef was a minute late or a couch cushion was out of place. I just knew he was mad at me, so I became defensive, snappy and irritable the instant he walked through the door. In my mind, I had failed to meet his unspoken expectations—I had failed as a wife and a mother—and I needed to stand up for myself.

But in truth, my poor husband was just happy to be home... well, until he saw my countenance. Then he assumed I was in a bad mood, perhaps mad at him, and this irritated him. This recipe for a perfect marriage regularly devolved into fights and silent stewing, leaving me feeling useless and more of a failure.

My feelings were false, of course; they were founded on a lie. However, because I chose to believe them, the enemy had a hay day messing with my confidence as a wife and mother. He put a huge wedge between Travis and me over stupid assumptions and false feelings.

The enemy is all about stirring false feelings. Therefore, it is critical that you (and I) "gird up the loins of your mind, be sober, and rest your hope fully upon the grace that is to be brought to you at the revelation of Jesus Christ" (1 Peter 1:13).

To *gird up the loins of your mind* means to prepare it for battle. Back when long tunics were all the rage for both men and women, they would have to tie up their skirts for battle before they charged into the fray. Neglecting to keep tabs on your wandering thoughts is like running into battle with your skirts flying. You'll trip and fall and everybody will see what's really underneath it all!

I want you to take a moment and pray. Ask God to reveal a moment in your life when you felt something that wasn't true—a time when the feeling was so strong that it changed the way you acted. Do you remember what that was like to have a false feeling take you to a place you never intended to go? Repent and ask the Lord to heal you of it.

SEEDING AND WEEDING

If it's tough for adults trying to be mothers and fathers, husbands and wives, imagine what it is like for our children in a world polluted with identity crises and false values.

Gender, race, social standing, victimhood and other identities are a major part of our culture today. The people who are choosing to walk out alternate identities feel that their chosen identity fits them better because of the way they feel. They *feel* that this is who they are. People cannot help feeling. We cannot be mad or hateful toward others for feeling something, but we can teach that feelings need to be aligned with truth. Feelings are not an absolute. They are one part of us, but not the whole part.

Feelings can be from a lie taking root or a dream being birthed. We need to be cautious because we can feel so strongly in either direction. We simply cannot "follow our hearts" or "trust our feelings" like so many great movies and books say we should do. Instead, we need to take all of our feelings and heart's desires to the Lord, sit under His care and let Him reveal truth. Without Him, "The heart is more deceitful than all else and is desperately sick; Who can understand it?" (Jeremiah 17:9).

What we do with a feeling makes all the difference. Our thoughts are powerful and our words more so. What we feed and water will grow and bear fruit.

This is why, as parents, we can't be afraid to unearth a seed planted by the enemy. Our job is to reveal it before it takes root. We do this by asking questions of our children; of being intentional about uncovering their underlying perspectives. We have to counteract the enemy's attack by being aware of our children's feelings and thought patterns. We need to dig into our children's soil so often that it's refreshing for them. And even though there may be times that tilling will be uncomfortable for all involved, it is vital that we do so.

In talking with our children, who will sin and stumble in the course of normal human feelings and experiences:

- we cannot be ruled by fear
- we cannot be self-righteous and religious like the Pharisees
- we cannot be so caught up in our own ideas that we miss God's design.

I think of how my teenage garden plant, Judea, responds to my weeding. He's pretty used to it by now, and God has taught me ways to communicate with him that are much less invasive for him than what I naturally do. Even so, there are times when I have allowed fear to enter in. Instead of a healthy weeding session, I smack into garden walls.

Weeding and Warring

To be successful for both the weeder and the weed-ee, our hearts as parents need to be right before God. Everything we do must be done with a heart to serve and love. Our actions must be for Jesus, in the Spirit of Jesus, and for our children's benefit, not our own ideals. The definition of real love is found in 1 Corinthians 13:4-7.

> *Love is patient and kind; love does not envy or boast; it is not arrogant or rude. It does not insist on its own way; it is not irritable or resentful; it does not rejoice at wrongdoing, but rejoices with the truth. Love bears all things, believes all things, hopes all things, endures all things.*

Loving our kids means leading them to Jesus with their feelings and identities. We all hope for our children to be great people. Many of us dreamed about our children long before they were a reality. As meaningful as these aspirations are, however, we cannot put our children in our box. God has plans for them that might not look at all like we envisioned. This is why the weeding we do needs to be done with God's plan in the forefront of our minds.

Plants will wilt when the weeds surrounding them are removed. This is because their root systems are shocked and there is no other covering for their leaves. The sun seems hotter, the water colder, but the covering of a weed is not true protection—it's deception. We need to weed and sift soil prayerfully, in love. If we do it often enough, it will be part of our nurturing routine and actually bring comfort to our kids. They will love having space and enjoy stretching toward Him. Plants flourish with the proper nutrition, space and sunshine, but they don't always feel that way at first.

If you have avoided weeding for a long, long time, you can't go in and rip weeds out that are entangled in the root system of your plant. (Recall our discussion of disciplining teenagers.) If that kind of weeding looks necessary because of neglect—perhaps the child was not always in your care—you must weed slowly, gently and with an abundance of caution. Be predictable, consistent, steady-handed and loving. Trust is crucial; it is imperative that you keep your word, so be thoughtful of what you say! You may also have to leave a few weeds until your "plant" is mature enough to make it through the process.

IT'S WORTH IT

Offenses will come, feelings based on lies the enemy has sown will arise, but diligence and regular tending will be enough. Jesus is enough. The Holy Spirit will never leave you or your children.

The importance of leading our children to honor the Lord, revering His ways above their feelings and desires, is critical to the survival of future generations. Always giving way to our children's feelings can greatly injure the chance of a Spirit-led future.

If you don't think this is serious, read 1 Samuel 2. Eli's sons had no reverence toward the Lord or His ways. Eli didn't hold them to it, either. Because of that, the Lord said both sons would die on the same day and that for generations there would be early death to their descendants among other horrible things—the results of lackadaisical parenting in the extreme.

How did things get so bad? Did Eli's sons suddenly decide one day to let all of God's ways fall to the wayside? No. This kind of dishonor and disobedience is formed over time. Eli was the head of his home and the priest before his sons ever became priests.

He was the example. He was the one responsible for holding his sons accountable. Eli had responsibilities to the people he was serving and to the Lord to teach and discipline his offspring—the future leaders of Israel. Tragically, he allowed his sons to give into their whims and cultivate their evil desires, and the consequences were heavy.

We as parents need to guard our children's hearts. We need to return to truth when our emotions get the best of us.

Of course, it is easier to tell other people what to do with their kids than to parent my own because I am emotionally attached to mine. Without the Lord, I want to give in to their emotions and indulge my own as well. But the cost is not worth it! There's an African proverb on child rearing: "It takes a village." I believe it. I need Jesus and those who love me enough to be honest enough to tell me what I'm missing in my life! We as parents can be blinded by offense, but far too often the enemy's blindfold is that discipline will injure lasting relationships. That's a painful twist of the truth that leads to destruction.

Feelings cannot rule the day; truth needs to rule. God is with us. He will reveal faults in our emotions. He is so good to uncover the enemy's lies.

Regularly come to Him. Regularly align with Him. Remember that spotlight I spoke of earlier? Remember you don't have to see everything. He will reveal it as you come under His care, His light. He will not fail you.

Make sure that your character is free from the love of money, being content with what you have; for He Himself said, "I will never desert you, nor will I ever forsake you."

Hebrews 13:5

CHAPTER DISCUSSION QUESTIONS

1. In what ways are you instilling truth and identity into your children?
2. In what ways have you sown insecurity?
3. How are you teaching your children to fight?
4. What false feelings have you given into that looking back were clearly lies from the enemy?
5. Now that you recognize them for what they are, how are you going about forgiveness, repentance, etc.?
6. Are you regularly weeding your own garden and your children's?
7. Are you finding your weeds and your children's weeds look the same?
8. How does that prepare you to war for them?
9. What are you watering yourself with? Your spouse? Your children?
10. Have you seen any fruit yet with your consistency, or do you need to work on that? *Look for it!* Sometimes there is more fruit than you think because human nature is to focus on the work and the trial. Look hard, daily, for fruit and beauty in your journey! It will change the level of joy you experience!

7

For and With

Do not lay up for yourselves treasures on earth, where moth and rust destroy and where thieves break in and steal; but lay up for yourselves treasures in heaven, where neither moth nor rust destroy and where thieves do not break in and steal. For where your treasure is, there your heart will be also.

Matthew 6:19-21

WE NEED TO BE FOR OUR CHILDREN and also *with* our children, not for our children *or* with our children. Oftentimes, we end up living in one condition or the other and we feel like we have to choose for the sake of time. Even though we tell ourselves that what we are doing is for the benefit of our children, we truly need to evaluate what we are calling a benefit.

Whether we work full-time or stay at home doesn't matter. It really is not the issue! We just need to be intentional with our time. If we do work full-time, is the payoff worth it? Do we need to work endless hours away from our children, leaving them to be raised by others, squeezing in a few hours a day so they can have cool things? Play more sports? Take piano lessons? Perhaps so our family can look like we have it all together? Is the extra income really needed at this time?

Now, I'm not talking about the job(s) that provide necessities and occasional treats for the family. I am a firm believer in hard work and sacrifices to lay a foundation for the next generation. It is good to earn a living, do well for yourself and your loved ones, and be successful financially. However, I feel the need to be extremely direct because the culture we live in is opposed to this idea of being for *and* with our children.

Our culture (American) says we are never enough. If our kids aren't wearing designer clothes and have the latest in technology, toys, gear, education, athletics and musical training, then somehow, we're failing them. Our culture teaches that we must give our children everything and withhold nothing.

Can I just say STOP! Those are lies! Such lies! Really, are children somehow worth less without the latest smartphone? No! So why do we get sucked into it?

Certainly, our children can have nice things. Our kids can wear name brands, and if you can give them the latest smartphone, great! And please, find the best violin teacher, the best soccer team, the best teaching tools... the best... *we can afford!*

Knowing what we can afford starts with knowing the true cost of the things we are striving to provide. What is time worth? Is your job or your wife's job only providing extras? If your kids are in school and it is not a sacrifice for you to work for all the extras, perfect. But if your kids are young and not yet in school, what exactly are you sacrificing?

Our kids need food, clothing, four walls and a roof that doesn't leak in the rain. They need a home! Those are some things we can't give up, but what are we sacrificing to earn extra income? Are they things we don't really need? Can we have joy in the little things while our littles are young enough to not demand our car keys or credit card?? (fixing that before you ever get there) If it comes to it, are color crayons and cardboard boxes enough for their joy and development? So many memories are made with parent and child working with simple tools rather than a child alone with an I-Phone 78. I know it sounds extreme, ridiculous, perhaps a bit invasive to your personal choices as a parent, but we should evaluate it.

We all know what a job provides: income, prestige, satisfaction (if it's a good one), but let's consider the cost of a job. Let's write it out, and not just the benefits, but the expenses. How much in childcare? How much in work clothes? Do you need your nails done? Haircuts? Special equipment? Do you buy more coffee and meals out because you work? It's nice to be able to do that for yourself, I agree. I definitely buy more coffee when I'm on the go!

Then there are the emotional costs. Many times, moms end up working to pay for childcare and maybe a little extra a month. Is that worth having someone else raise your child for 8 to 12 hours a day? Are they instilling values into your child's heart like you can? What values are being taught simply by going to work instead of staying home?

As a mom who has both stayed home and worked, I know the emotional challenges of each role. Though there is a particular level of nerve grating that can happen when at home, we need to recognize the attraction of working outside the home as well.

Let's be honest. It can, in a way, be easier to send your kids to childcare and head off to work than to stay home all day trying to train children. And I don't say that lightly! Yet, it is also emotionally difficult to say goodbye and head to work in the morning, then return home in the evening to deal with the behaviors learned at daycare.

Kids are crazy and can be very taxing. They are constant work, no breaks, and they only seem to want us when they get in trouble or need something. The break we do get is spent cleaning up their ridiculous messes.

At work, unless the job conditions are terrible, we are usually appreciated, our efforts are recognized, and we get to have adult conversation. At home, we often work with little to no sleep and barely have time to shower. We cook and serve little people all day and for what? Complaining, whining, nerve-grating attitudes! We're constantly told we are doing a terrible job, either by our kids refusing to eat or the enemy screaming in our ears that we are failing. There is little visible glory in being a stay-at-home parent.

Now, I realize that I could turn these last two paragraphs around, change "at work" to "at home" and get the same number of heads nodding in agreement. Nurses rarely get to take a break on a 12-hour shift. School teachers often feel undervalued. I know moms and dads who struggle in their jobs and would love to be at home with their kids but need the income. The point is, there is an attraction to being away, and sometimes that attraction can be used by the enemy.

Today, society applauds the career parent, especially women. In the name of equal rights and empowerment, moms can feel less than successful if they're not holding down a gig as a CEO of a multinational corporation while raising six kids on a farm and canning corn and green beans on the weekend.

This explains the intense looks I received when I told people I homeschooled my kids, or even when I was a stay-at-home mom. They came with an accusatory essence that vomited "loser." Through their clenched teeth, I often heard, "I could never do that."

Oh no? Why not?

For and With

There is a very real war against us staying home to raise our children. Our culture, including our financial needs, are against us. The enemy wants nothing more than to steal our God-given right to raise our children in the way that they should go. He wants us to live with internal conflict that robs us at both ends—professionally and domestically. He further wants to destroy our ability to be at home by attacking the very foundation that makes it possible—the two-parent family. Of course, I applaud and support my single-parent friends. Theirs is not an easy life.

We all have to work in some capacity. Our jobs pay for the home, the food, the braces, pets and doctor visits. And if you're a single mom or dad, your job pays for everything. If that is you, rock this! You're going to make it! May God give you strength for every moment to be full of intentionality and gratitude!

The traditional roles of one parent working outside the home so the other can work at home is a bit outdated, and it's so sad to me. I am thankful women get to work. I am all for that, but I am also saddened by the fact that now many have to work just to make ends meet. I do wish I could afford to be a stay at home mom and wife, but it's not possible for me. I am so grateful for the sacrifices we made when our children were little, because of them a great foundation of training was laid. I understand that most families need to have two incomes. I simply want to put a spotlight on the why (Why is it that we work?), and make sure the why is worth it. I want to deeply evaluate what we're paying for and at what cost?

Life is crazy hard without this struggle, but we've got to address it. If there is a way to do it, the best situation for your children is one parent at home, and if you truly cannot be there, don't stress. God has it! Just be intentional with the time you do have.

TIME ON THE FLOOR

How, and how often I interact with my children helps shape them into the adults they're destined to be. Every single day we spend with our children is an opportunity to demonstrate what is valuable.

I am *for* my children. Most parents I know share the same devotion. Every bone in my body longs to give them the best of everything in this world. Sadly, this obsession has become a war within myself. I want to provide it all, but time is cruel, short and easily taken for granted. We need to be *for* our children, but we also desperately need to be *with* them.

One of my favorite books on parenting boys is *Mother & Son, The Respect Effect*, by Emerson Eggerichs. He writes about the deception of Eve. I had contemplated how Eve wanted good things, but he points out the attitude in her heart to get them. She wanted to be more like God. She wanted wisdom and knowledge and so, she aggressively went after them in a way God never intended. Indeed, God forbade it. Yet in her obsession for good, despite what God said was true, she decided the forbidden tree was good after all, that it was worth it. In her mind, it had to lead to a good thing, but she never thought about God's design, the sacrifice, the obedience, the true priority or the consequences. In a word, she *rationalized*.

We do that far too often when evaluating our childrearing. God's word gives so many ideas on how to pour into our kids, yet we twist them to justify creating pictures on empty canvases, scenes never meant for our children.

What, you might ask, do I mean by that?

Does your child *really* want to play soccer? Study the violin? Go to survival camp in the French Alps and live off caterpillars?

For and With

Are your goals for you or your children? Are they things you've prayed about and sought God on? Or do you want your child to have all the opportunities and choices you never had?

Parents, we need to pray and obey, lay a foundation of faith, hope and love. We need to place our children's feet firmly on the Rock of Salvation. We need to let God paint their canvases through our hands. We need to surrender the brush.

Eve wanted something good. We all want something good. Isn't fruit grown from good seed, nurtured and well kept, something good? If we want healthy, lifelong relationships with our children, sharing their lives and thriving in the fruit of the Spirit, shouldn't we be sowing into our relationships with them and their spiritual growth instead of feeding only their earthly desires or worse—our earthly desires for them?

I am a dreamer. Sometimes I dream of what could be and I lose all sight of what is now. I struggle with this war every day. I want to give my children everything I can imagine. I want my children to have what I had as a kid. I want my kids to go further and do more than I did. In these wants, I grow evermore distracted in providing those things. Rather than nurturing the seedlings in my home, I hyper-focus on the preparation for their future, one I've built in my mind with little regard to what God has for them right now.

In my obsession, I build, work and till the ground outside to prepare for the future of my little seedlings that aren't even strong enough to be outdoors yet. And although I am doing good work, I need to be balanced because this intense outdoor building can distract me and cause me to forget to water what I already have inside—those budding little plants thirsty for my attention right now.

For and With

Sometimes I think we till and prep for types of plants we don't even have, but in our minds, we see them as we want them. So, we cut into our pliant little ones, grafting in our hopes to grow fruit they were never meant to bear.

We cannot grow what we do not sow. And really, with our children, God hands us our seeds and we are then responsible to grow them without fully knowing what they will grow into. We need to ask the Lord how to care for the plants He's given us because what we feed our fledglings better be specific to their design or it can destroy them.

Are you so caught up in building your child's future that you're not feeding them where they're at now? Are you working too many hours just to provide things that are temporal? Have you even spent a moment to ask God what your child's future holds? Or how He wants you to sow?

No one can serve two masters; for either he will hate the one and love the other, or else he will be loyal to the one and despise the other. You cannot serve God and mammon.

Matthew 6:24

We need to get our priorities straight. I had a motto when the kids were little, and it was a war trying to stick to it. I often fell short, sacrificing time for meaningless things, but God was good and constantly brought me back.

My motto was:

I'd rather have my kids play with cardboard boxes and have me around than play with fancy toys without me.

Time is a cruel master. Don't let it rule. Instead, manage it well! (Same with money) We will never get this time back. Be intentional with it! Yes, work hard to provide great opportunities for your kids, but don't get so caught up in the opportunities that you lose sight of the fruit of the Spirit that you expect when they are grown. Fruit trees need shaping when they're young or they grow wild. They need pruning at the right time so that fruit will come in abundance. Just remember who owns the farm.

> *Do not be deceived, God is not mocked; for whatever a man sows, that he will also reap. For he who sows to his flesh will of the flesh reap corruption, but he who sows to the Spirit will of the Spirit reap everlasting life. And let us not grow weary while doing good, for in due season you will reap if we do not lose heart.*
>
> Galatians 6:7-9

When I think of a wealthy person with no moral compass or ability for true companionship, I imagine them miserable and making others the same. When I think of how I am when I am stressed, rushed, pressured by this world to "get it all done," I am miserable and so are those around me. I want my children to grow into good people. We need to "sow what we want to grow," as my pastor, Jeff Ecklund, so often says.

In Matthew 4, after Jesus was baptized, He was led to the wilderness to be tempted. And what did Satan use to tempt Him? The devil knew he was hungry so he tempted Him with food and justified it with scripture. Made sense, right? "Hey Jesus, you're hungry. Turn these rocks into bread."

The devil continued to twist scripture two more times to tempt Jesus with things that were enticing. To be tempting at all, what Satan used seemed like a good thing, even for just a moment. Kind of like what Eve heard. "What's wrong with a little knowledge, Eve? God doesn't want you to be dumb. And neither does Adam."

It's like that for us. Extra work for the church can be a good thing. Extra help for a neighbor in need can be a good thing. Taking on another part-time job to pay for extras can be a good thing—pay off the car, get a new house, maybe go on that vacation that you've needed for a decade. These things can bring life and blessing but it all needs to be in obedience and freedom of the Lord and kept in balance.

There are times when you just need to do something extra because it's the right thing to do. Yet in our culture, we are so caught up in obligations that we have lost what is truly important. Obligations end up putting our children on the altar of sacrifice. What are we gaining? More to the point, what are we losing? The cost is evident on our newsfeed.

Count the cost. *The true cost.* Again, every family is different and designed uniquely by the Lord. You have to pray and obey. You have to talk with the Lord about what is right for your family. I can't decide that for you, and I'm not saying to you work or don't work. Working parents have advantages and disadvantages. I know; I am a working mom, and it is very difficult finding time for appointments, fighting guilt and shuffling my schedule when the kids are sick. However, God is *always* good. I know this is where God has my family, and because I know, I have complete confidence and peace. When hard times or attack comes, the enemy has no ground.

Seek the Lord. Seek his peace. Be for and with your children!

> *You will go out in joy*
> *and be led forth in peace;*
> *the mountains and hills*
> *will burst into song before you,*
> *and all the trees of the field*
> *will clap their hands.*
>
> Isaiah 55:12

For and With

CHAPTER DISCUSSION QUESTIONS

1. Ask the Lord if you are where He wants you to be for your family.
2. What did he reveal? Write it in your journal.
3. Are you sacrificing your time with your kids unnecessarily?
4. What is it that tempts you? Why do you think that is?
5. Do you feel that you're failing your children if you don't give them what you hope to?
6. Are you really failing them? Why or why not?
7. Are there any areas that you need to give up?
8. Do you need to be more intentional with your time at home, more purposeful?
9. Note: intentional, purposeful time can happen while you do the laundry, dishes, or other chores. Our willingness to slow down and enjoy it makes all the difference.

8

My Crucible Moment

WE CREATE OUR OWN FUTURES. God is faithful and will direct our steps if we let Him, but our choices directly affect our futures. Ironically, "we want God's outcome but we don't always want His process" (Stephen Alkire). Yet His process is intended to prepare us for our future in Him. This is because:

Yesterday's faith won't get you through tomorrow's crisis.

Stephen Alkire

God once asked me the hardest question of my life, "If I take Eden home, will you still love Me?"

I started to cry as I typed that. That time of my life is when fear and doubt began to stir around me; when my promised land was first questioned; when drought was felt for the first time. And yet it made me all that I am today. It was my greatest test, my crucible, and it taught me one thing: That God is a god of His Word. I could not have learned it any other way.

Like Abram, God had spoken to me. He gave me a hope and a future (ref. Jeremiah 29:11). He told me what my future can hold. He gave me some insight into all that was coming. And like Abram, God has had to remind me of who I am time and time again. He has had to show me what being His daughter looks like and that He thinks I'm worth it. I sometimes struggle with accepting the love He has for me. I have struggled, as Moses did, believing I am enough for what He made me to do and that what He's saying to me will actually come to pass. Yet I know that I AM has my life and the lives of my children in the palm of His mighty hand.

> *Moses said to God, "Suppose I go to the Israelites and say to them, 'The God of your fathers has sent me to you,' and they ask me, 'What is his name?' Then what shall I tell them?"*
>
> *God said to Moses, "I AM who I am. This is what you are to say to the Israelites: 'I AM has sent me to you.'"*
>
> Exodus 3:13-14

I am finally at a place where I believe God. I trust His plan for me. I trust that He is who He says He is and that He made me with a plan and purpose in His heart. He finds joy in me. It makes Him angry when I doubt my worth that He paid for with the life of His Son. Still, He's not angry at me. He gets angry because He has so much in store for me. For me to do and be what He created me for, I have to believe I am who I AM says I am.

It has been a long journey. It's not over. But I believe. I trust His process.

EDEN'S FALL

It was a sunny day and I was up early to bake a batch of bread for a big event at church. We had a small two-bedroom house with no hallways. It had been built in sections starting in the 1920s and resuming every couple of decades when the present owners found the money and the will. There were no hallways; every room connected to another room, a human maze. I often thought they should have just torn it down and started afresh.

That morning, I had my hair thrown atop my head, sporting my "home only" lounge attire, and I was working hard to get everything done. My kids were playing at my feet and I had lost track of time.

Eden, my sweet 22-month-old girl, was getting whiney. I realized it was past lunchtime. I threw together some peanut butter and jelly and set her in her highchair next to Judea who was four at the time. They ate while I baked.

Looking up, I saw four men and some boys walking up my driveway. Now, we had huge kitchen windows, and I was in a spaghetti strap tank top—nothing I wanted these men to see me in! As I ran around the corner into my laundry room to hide, I told Travis who was coming up the driveway. He said they were there to help him change out our windshield. *Gee, thanks for the warning, Travis!* He went outside to greet them. I thought for a second, weighing my options, looked over at Eden and Judea eating peacefully at the table and decided to go for it.

Eden was almost potty trained and could get in and out of her highchair on her own. I told the kids that I'd be right back, then ran to the bathroom to take the fastest Navy shower of my life and throw on "public appropriate" clothes. I was lathered up and just about to rinse when I heard the crash and crying. Judea came running into my bathroom yelling, "Mommy, Eden fell down and I think she's hurt!"

My heart lurched. I told him to run and get Dad. The giant windows were still open and I was now less presentable than before. As I scrambled to get out, Judea ran back in to tell me that he couldn't get Dad's attention. I threw towels over myself and rushed to the kitchen. From the time I stepped into the shower until I ran out soggy and soapy took about three minutes but it seemed like a lifetime.

My Crucible Moment

Wrapped like a cheap Cleopatra, I got to the kitchen to find Eden whimpering and standing next to a kitchen chair. She wasn't crying but was obviously upset about whatever had just happened.

I looked her over, hugged her and asked, "Are you ok?"

"Yeah," she answered with a little sniffle.

I began to question her and Judea as to what in the world happened. Eden had fallen from her highchair somehow. Still worried about flashing the men on the other side of the glass, I stayed crouched and focused on my girl and any possible injury. I sat her up on the table and looked her over thoroughly. She had a bruise forming on her leg but nothing else. I asked her if she bumped her head. She said no.

Now, I was raised in the back of an ambulance, quite literally, because my mom was a paramedic. I had been to more EMT classes in my life than most EMTs. I know how to check for head injury. I was worried because Eden was born with two different sized pupils—a common symptom of a head injury but normal for her. Unless other symptoms began, I'd have no reason to suspect further damage.

I saw that she was fine. No real injuries to speak of. She was way overdue for nap time and I needed to get the drying soap off me, so I scooped her up in my arms and carried her to my bathroom to stay with me while I showered off and dressed. I knew she was ready for sleep but still agitated from the fall. We ended up sitting on my bathroom floor, rocking her in my arms, and she was asleep in less than a minute.

I thought it odd how quickly she fell asleep, but then again, she was way over-tired so I disregarded it and laid her in bed.

Back in the kitchen, I finished up the bread, switched loaves in the oven and endeavored to be a polite hostess to the men who were here to help us. They seemed much less invasive now. With all that was going on, I never once looked over at the highchair.

When Eden woke up from her nap, she was crying and fussy; it was an annoyed or sick cry. She sometimes fussed like this when she woke up and had to go potty but was too tired to articulate it. I took her to the bathroom. She was dry, so I sat her up on the toilet and tried to love on her and sweet talk her out of her mood while we waited for nature to take its course.

That's when everything erupted. Eden looked at me blankly and then vomited her lunch all over me. I knew this wasn't normal sickness. The odd moments of the day had built my stress level to breaking. Amidst the puke and fear, I called out to Travis for help. He came running. I explained it all in a stream of conscious yelling. Fortunately, Travis is a fast listener. As he held Eden, I called our doctor.

THE STORM

Normally I wouldn't worry about a toddler vomiting, but I knew deep inside that something was terribly wrong. I also sensed the enemy sowing fear. He had waited for God's intuition to alert me to Eden's condition, then he jumped to distort it. Fear entered my heart and I thought about vaccines and the horrible reactions kids were having, some fatal. I did a quick calculation. It was Saturday and Eden got hers on Thursday.

Was she just now reacting?

On the phone with Doctor Chang, my thoughts were interrupted and I said, "Oh my word, she fell out of her highchair before her nap! What if she has a concussion?!"

Doctor Chang reassured me, "Calm down, Morgan. If she does have a concussion, she'll throw up again. If that happens, bring her in to the ER and we'll look her over."

I felt a lump in my throat. My heart was racing. *How could I have missed a concussion?* I looked her over so well. There wasn't even a red spot or bump anywhere on her head. I had triple-checked her because of how her pupils belie the normal symptoms. *Why did I leave her alone?* Yes, Travis was in the vicinity and could see her, but nothing in my brain at this point was logical. I was a mess.

My panic exploded when Eden threw up again. I'd seen enough. I hollered for Travis to grab her diaper bag. I wrapped her in a towel, and we flew to the ER at Newport Hospital. Eden was lethargic and beginning to go limp. I felt helpless, responsible, guilty. I kept saying to myself that she could get in and out of her highchair on her own. *How did she fall?*

The ER was jammed, chaotic and understaffed. We had to wait and wait. The longer we sat, the worse Eden became. Yet, she wasn't a priority to them. Just a head injury, possibly a concussion. But no one really looked. They were too busy. *Just like I had I been?*

Finally, my normally reserved Travis caught the attention of a nurse and made it clear that we were going to be seen one way or another! He's a man with a naturally strong presence, and when his family is threatened, he's been known to take on giants.

By now my head was spinning. Eden was now barely waking up when she vomited. The desk nurse was so overwhelmed she just stared into her computer and asked us questions and typed the answers. She never looked up at Eden. I wanted to shake her. But she was the nurse. Besides, I was probably being too dramatic for the situation. I was panicked; I knew I shouldn't be. I was shaking so bad. I wanted them to actually look at her!

That's when Martha Winje, one of my favorite people in the world, entered the room. I had known Martha since I was four years old. She started out as one of my mom's students and was now a Physician's Assistant (P.A.). Martha took one look at Eden, shot an annoyed glance toward the nurse and got things moving. She could tell something wasn't right. The way Eden was throwing up was not normal for a concussion. She was too lethargic. Something worse was presenting. Martha comforted me with her familiar voice, saying they were going to do a CAT scan, but since Eden was so young, they had to call the children's hospital to ensure they did it properly.

Time was moving at half speed. I had tunnel vision. My focus was intensely on the face of my baby. We did the scan, and as I sat in the examining room waiting for results, I held Eden in my arms and prayed. Martha returned with a genuine look of concern in her eyes. She took a deep breath and spoke words I never thought I'd hear.

"Morgan, we got the results back from the scan. Your daughter has a brain bleed and we need to fly her to Spokane to the children's hospital. We're not neurologists and we don't know how bad the bleed is. We'll give her a sedative to keep her calm on the way and keep the pressure down. But... we don't know if she'll make it to Spokane."

I broke.

"It's my fault. I left her for a minute. I shouldn't have left her!"

As I sobbed, Martha sat next to me and put her hand on my knee.

"Morgan," she said softly, "You're a good mom. We've all walked away at some point. It could have happened to any of us; it just ended up being you this time. It's not your fault. She could have fallen with you in the room."

Her words brought some comfort and a glimmer of reason, but my thoughts were blurred by irrational blame. Even in the kitchen, I hadn't been fully present. I was baking. I was embarrassed by my attire. I was focused on getting things done and making myself presentable. Blame, guilt and fear gripped me. I wept and shook uncontrollably.

FLIGHT TO LIFE

The next thing I knew, we were in the main ER room. I had pulled myself together enough to focus on comforting my baby girl. Nurses finally mobilized. They were trying to get an IV into Eden's tiny arm and were failing over and over. Doctor Chang had arrived by now. Clearly, the nurses had waited too long to get Eden on fluids. She was so dehydrated that they couldn't get a vein.

Dr. Chang snapped at the nurses: "You're done. Don't touch her again! We'll let the professionals do it when they get here!"

He was speaking of Life Flight. His words were still echoing when they rushed in. Suddenly, there were so many people hovering around my terrified baby Eden. She was exhausted and screaming. I knew she shouldn't have been crying; it meant brain pressure was building up, possibly fatally. I tried to soothe her, to keep myself from exploding, anything to help. I wanted to vomit. I wanted everything to stop.

They got her IV going and gave her a sedative to make her sleep on the flight to Spokane. I asked if I could ride with her. I knew from my life with a paramedic mom that one family member could go. I wanted to be by Eden's side if she didn't make it. I didn't want her to leave this earth terrified next to a stranger.

All this time, Travis stood by me. I felt so guilty, a failure of a mom. I could barely look at him. It was hard to focus on how he felt at this moment, watching helplessly as professionals applied all they knew just to keep his daughter alive. Yet I just knew I had to be with Eden and I said so. Somewhere in the din, I heard Travis say "Go. I'll follow in the car and...."

We were out the door before he finished.

They rolled Eden out to the roof as I followed, sick and unstable in my footing. They put her in the back and led me to the front with the pilot. I didn't know that I'd have to ride up front. I had never actually seen anyone get into the helicopter up close. I was always at a distance. He gave me a headset so we could talk. I didn't want to talk. I wanted to see my baby girl. I wanted to hold her hand.

In the headset, I could hear what was happening in the back. Eden was in hysterics. She was terrified. I couldn't see her. I couldn't touch her. I couldn't tell her I was there. All she knew is that strangers were hovering over her and mom and dad were nowhere to be found. The sedative wasn't working. She was supposed to be sleeping, relaxed, not screaming. All I could think about was that she had to stop crying or she could die. The word *die* lingered in my mind.

We lifted off and shot straight toward Spokane. I had been in a helicopter before but never at night. They don't fly with headlights. Darkness enveloped us as we left the illumination of our small town. The pilot tried to make small talk. I was polite but wanted him to shut up. Eden was crying so hard. With every sob, my heart sank a little deeper. *What if she stops? What if she doesn't make it?* I stopped myself and went back to prayer. I was forcing myself to bring every thought captive, (ref. 2 Corinthians 10:5) but fear chased me. I had been praying the whole time but fear is a great interrupter.

The stars were so bright. It felt strange to slice through the night sky with no light to lead the way. In my heart, I cried out to God. I begged Him to protect Eden, to give us and everyone driving a safe trip. I prayed for safe travel for Travis. He had Judea in the car and would be speeding to rendezvous with us. I knew he was scared too.

In a moment of panicked prayer, as the brightest star in the sky caught my eye, God spoke to me.

"I used a star to show the Wisemen where the Savior was born. His birth was a miracle. He rose from the dead. He saved you. Look, I am here. I am with you. Don't worry, have peace!"

Flying through the nightmarish sky as my baby fought for life just beyond my grasp, God met me. Until then, I felt alone, drenched in guilt. Now, my darkness gave way to the light within me, a light that once heralded a new world and would do so again.

ANGELS OF MERCY

Deep in prayer and armed with truth, we arrived at Sacred Heart Hospital. The wave of emotions nearly drowned me. Eden was still crying but she made it this far. Hospital staff ran to us. They only run when it's urgent, when it's life or death. Eden reached for me. I ran next to her gurney and into the hospital.

My father-in-law was already at the hospital visiting someone else and was waiting inside the doors from the roof when we burst through. *Praise God for a familiar face.*

I had held everything together for Eden, but once inside, it was like starting over. A new ER, a new round of questions and another check-in process. I wanted to remove people's heads.

You said my baby might die. Why the questions? Why the delay? Why does this process seem to go on forever?

I was emotionally drained but still ready for battle if only I knew the territory. I couldn't win this alone. Thankfully, we were at a place equipped for this kind of emergency.

Amidst the fresh chaos, Travis arrived looking as worried as I felt. It was rare to see helplessness on his face.

After all the poking and torture at Newport Hospital, now Sacred Heart needed a bigger IV and some blood work. They kept impaling my kicking and screaming daughter, trying to find a vein in her withered limbs. I'd had enough. Looking up at Travis, I asked him to stay with Eden for a minute. I had to breathe. I couldn't lose it in front of her.

I walked out into the hall looking for a bathroom, any place to hide. Guilt for having to leave sat like a hard, painful lump in my throat. The bathroom was next to a small waiting room. As I rounded the corner, everyone stood up. It was full of my family. My brother-in-law looked deep into my eyes, brokenhearted, searching for hope. I had none to spare. He asked how I was doing; how Eden was doing. Fighting for air, I managed an "OK" and pushed past him and into the bathroom.

I closed and locked the door, leaned hard against it and tried to get a breath. Looking into the mirror, I gave myself a "pull it together" talk. Through my tunnel vision, everything was surreal. Staring at myself, I spoke to the Lord. "I'm sorry, I just can't do it! I can't keep it together anymore! I need You!"

I collapsed to the floor and wept uncontrollably for about five minutes. I knew people could hear me. I didn't want to make it harder on them, and my mind said. *They're probably thinking this was my fault.*

I went to the toilet to vomit. *Was this my fault?* I dry heaved and gave up. I had to get back to Eden. I had to be what she needed.

I pulled myself up by the sink base. It took all my strength. I felt wobbly and nauseous. I leaned heavily over the cold porcelain and washed my face, forced myself through the fog and back to Eden's room. I didn't even notice the silent faces of my family as I passed.

All the poking was done and they scheduled an MRI of Eden's brain. In the interim, I got to be alone with Eden. I soaked in every minute with her. I studied her face, her tiny hands. I never wanted to forget.

The MRI was done in a big empty room with only the machine and the gurney. It filled the room with noise. It was late and we were all tired. The doctors told me to do whatever I could to keep her calm and put her to sleep. So, I sang to her like I did every night at home. It was a song our pastors had recently taught us. I loved it. It was the song of my heart at the time.

I will enter Your gates with thanksgiving in my heart
Come into your courts to bring You praise.

I worshipped as I sang to her, brushing her hair back, sliding my hand against her smooth, chubby cheeks. She calmed and slept for the test. That was such a sweet moment the Lord gave me. I had peace because I chose to be thankful when I didn't know the outcome. I was thankful for the moment.

The neurologist we had that night was a younger, dark-haired man. I can't recall his name but I remember his plaid shirt and black vest, his calm and sweet demeanor.

After the test results came back, he came to the room, leaned casually against the heater by the window and said words I needed so badly and will never forget.

"Someone must have been looking out for your little girl. Her brain bleed was not caused by trauma. It is an aneurysm. If she wouldn't have fallen, her brain would have bled anyway. She still would have started throwing up and every doctor would have said 'stomach bug, send her home,' and she would have died."

Not caused by trauma. Not my fault? I didn't really take that in. The words hit my shell of blame and guilt and ran down to the floor.

He asked if she had ever been sick before. There was only one time she had ever thrown up in her life before that. He said it looked like her brain had bled once before and that was probably the time. He said it was a miracle that she was alive and that this bleed hadn't changed much since her first scan in Newport. He felt she'd be stable through the night. They'd do more tests in the morning to find the cause of her aneurysm.

Will You...?

The night was far spent. The PICU didn't allow parents to stay in their children's rooms. One parent could sit by their child's bedside in a blue vinyl covered recliner, but the other had to leave. Travis said I could go rest. I didn't want to but I had gotten to fly to be with her. It was his turn to be with Eden for a while.

The hospital allowed us to sleep across the skywalk in the sleeping rooms provided for the doctors and nurses. The rooms had twin beds and an alarm clock on a small nightstand. It felt like a cell. I still felt I belonged there.

I sat in that room in the dark and went over everything. I was praying and crying out to God when He interrupted me sternly.

"If I take Eden home, will you still love Me?"

In that moment, I had a decision to make. Was my God truly my God? Did I trust Him fully? Did I truly choose Him no matter what? I had to be honest with myself and search my heart.

I quietly and honestly answered, "Yes."

As I sobbed, I was reminded that both of my children were His anyway, that really, I get to borrow them and am meant to raise them to be His from the beginning. That brought such a deep peace. I knew He knew better. I couldn't control this. I couldn't will an outcome. I could only be honest and quiet and know that He is God. I knew that He knows better than I do. He knew what her future would hold if she lived. He knew what this world needed to come to know Him. She loved Him. She knew Him. I had to face the fact that I knew where she'd go if she left this world, and that I would see her again one day.

O death, where is your victory? O death, where is your sting?

1 Corinthians 15:55

God can use these heart-wrenching moments to grip the lost. His love runs deep. He wants nothing more than for all to be with Him for eternity, and if a child coming home at a young age ensured their eternity with Him, well then....

I decided to submit fully, no matter His decision. If this would bring others to their knees and lead to their eternity in Heaven, then so be it. More so, if this would ensure her eternity, so be it.

I chose to trust and let go.

I was quietly weeping, shaking, and exhausted, but I had a deep peace. God's presence was all around me. I was enveloped in a love so deep, so tangible, that nothing could withstand it, not even fear.

I laid there in the black. Time flowed slowly. I felt every second. My thoughts were toward my Savior, listening for His Word. It seemed a long time but more like a hug full of anticipation. Finally, He spoke softly to me,

"She's going to be OK. You're going to get to raise your little girl."

Wrapped in the arms of my Father, hope anchoring my heart, I slept.

Morning Has Broken

The next day the testing began. More MRI's and a new neurologist. He was tall, strong and confident with fiery red hair and a terrific posture. (I don't know why that helped, but it did.) I was thrilled and honored to meet the man God was using to heal my daughter. What a man he is!

We waited for results; it seemed like forever. The big question was whether it was a tumor that caused her aneurysm or a vascular malformation (AVM). The doctor hoped for an AVM because those are typically a one-time event, while tumors could mean cancer or multiple surgeries.

My Crucible Moment

We prayed and God answered. It was an AVM—basically a cluster of veins taking up an eighth of her brain that had formed improperly in utero. The veins in that area had skipped the capillary stage. They went from large arterial veins to tiny veins. This caused pressure to build up and led to an aneurism. We were so thankful it wasn't a tumor, but the road was far from over.

She had to have surgery. There were a few hard things that my peanut had to go through to prepare for surgery. The first was an arterial IV. The doctors tried to put one through her groin area, only to fail repeatedly. I was so tired of seeing my baby get poked and bleed all over again, so Travis stayed with her. Since they couldn't get a good line in her groin, they had to go into her carotid artery in her neck. The tubing was more like a small hose and needle was huge! My strong husband had to take the lead for that one as well. It's a terrible thing to watch your child be tortured. I wanted to attack the people who were hurting my baby, but knew they were helping her. It just felt wrong. I can't imagine what God felt watching Jesus, knowing the end from the beginning, knowing that pain brings healing.

She also had to have an angiogram. This was to find exactly where and how much blood they were dealing with. Because her brain was still bleeding, the doctors had to call in a specialist from Seattle to do a potentially fatal procedure to try to stop the bleeding so she could have surgery. It was a strange position to be in. She had to have this life-threatening procedure to have life-saving surgery.

I leaned hard into God's promise, "You'll get to raise your little girl."

The way the procedure was explained to us in layman's terms was that the doctor would inject "glue" into Eden's veins. The hope was that the timing would be perfect and the glue would dry at the exact spot needed to stop all blood flow to the areas that they needed to remove in surgery. If it failed, there was a strong likelihood of stroke or death.

We had to sign release forms before they would proceed. We really had no choice. We signed and began to pray HARD, again.

Time passed. We waited. We prayed. When the doctor finally came out, his face made my heart sink. He looked stunned, pale, and he stuttered as he spoke.

"We have good news and only good news. I don't know what to say; this is so rare, and scientifically it doesn't make sense."

We all stood frozen, listening intently.

He went on to say that he didn't have to do the risky procedure, that somehow all blood flow to the area completely stopped. It isolated itself. No "glue" for Eden! We were all so excited to see God at work again. He kept meeting us, time and time again, miracle after miracle.

Can't Keep A Good Girl Down

The surgery was scheduled and the day came. We were back in anesthesia to put Eden to sleep before surgery. We as parents got to be with her, I assume to keep her as calm as possible. The anesthesiologist gave her some meds to put her out but moments later, she began to wake up. The PICU nurse was stunned as she watched Eden come out of anesthesia. The anesthesiologist gave Eden more meds to put her to sleep again, only to find that they weren't lasting either. They gave more, yet Eden kept waking up. I was beginning to get worried that she might wake up during surgery!

Before I knew it, we had 22 nurses and doctors surrounding Eden's bed, all of them blown away by this determined toddler. They'd given her enough medicine to put a 350lbs. man to sleep and there was my tiny Eden emerging from sleep and looking for breakfast.

That's when we all realized why the sedative in the helicopter didn't work. Eden metabolizes the medication at such a fast rate that she needs more than most. A lot more. The medical staff was stunned. Poor little thing. They finally got her to sleep and we went down to the surgical floor to meet up with her neurologist and send her on her way.

My mother in law had a vision while praying that it was going to be God's hands doing the surgery through our strong, red-headed neurologist. I already knew Eden would live. I already knew I'd get to raise her, but that brought even more peace to my heart.

We kissed her sweet face before they wheeled her away, and I cheerfully shook the doctor's hand and earnestly thanked him. I couldn't imagine doing his job. I couldn't imagine having that calling on my life.

Yet I had NO fear! I had NO doubt that she'd be fine. I trusted my God to keep His Word to me.

Travis and I took the elevator back to the waiting room floor. I was giddy with excitement. I knew the testimony to come. I felt it deep in my bones. God wanted to spread hope and joy to our friends and family in the waiting room. We visited with them as we waited. I laughed and encouraged others who were distraught with worry and paralyzed with fear.

I must have been a sight! Bubbly and joyful, I KNEW my girl was getting fixed up and would be fine. I was excited to be almost done! Not everyone had that peace.

The doctors told us Eden would likely be blind. Almost definitely in one eye, but likely both. The area they had to remove was in the area of vision. That was hard to accept, but she would be alive and overall healthy.

The surgery went well and everything was taken care of. Eden was kept under anesthesia during the first stage of her recovery. We didn't know if she was blind or how everything else turned out for a few days. Adding to our wait, she had to be on a ventilator and have no stimulation during the first few days. I wanted to hold her and kiss her but we weren't supposed to touch her or talk to her.

Travis and I clung together. We left and went out to eat and bought things we needed at the hospital as a distraction. Just taking a shower felt strange. *Wasn't it a shower that started all this?* I felt weird no matter what I did. Nothing felt right. I knew I had to take care of myself and be balanced, but I was a stranger in a strange land. I ached to see my son, Judea, who was staying with my amazing in-laws, and I wanted my daughter to be well. Life was a blur.

When Eden was finally allowed to wake up, the doctors made sure she was stable and then moved her to the pediatric oncology ward for the rest of her recovery. They said even though she didn't have cancer, it was a clean area and she was less likely to get sick from another patient while trying to recover.

Oh, and the great news? She wasn't blind.

Eden can see!

THE SIEGE WORKS

I felt I had made it through Eden's ordeal with great faith. That is until the second to the last day in the hospital. We were getting ready to head home and Eden started to throw up again. My heart skipped. The lump in my throat returned. Fear and I held an impromptu reunion. *What if?* stirred.

The throwing up turned out to be a reaction to one of her medications, but the effect on me was far worse. For the first time, fear actually gripped me. Previously, it had been lingering, making sharp jabs but never fully latching on. Now it dug into my soul with claws sharp and quick. I was seeing the road to Eden's recovering and wondering how long, how far, how rough this would be. I wasn't prepared for this part of the journey.

OK, Lord, I know you said I'd get to raise her, but what do we have to go through? Are we going to be in a constant state of tests and hospitals? Am I going to have to watch her get poked and prodded the rest of her life?

The pediatric oncology ward was a hard place to be in. I felt guilty knowing my daughter was going home. Other parents sat by their kiddos fighting for their lives—moms and dads watching their kids puke, lose hair and fade into death when all else failed.

What kind of fears did these parents face? How would they get through it without Jesus holding them? Fear was made very real to me in that place. The spirit loomed there, waiting for those it could devour.

> *For God has not given us a spirit of fear, but of power, love, and a sound mind*
>
> 2 Timothy 1:7

Fear is a spirit. Unfortunately, the spirit of fear loves the children's hospital. It invaded me in that moment when Eden threw up, and it clung to my back for years like a gargoyle on a castle wall, waiting for the worst moments to whisper horrible thoughts, robbing the peace God had for me and filling me with doubt.

Sure, you'll get to raise Eden... in abject horror the whole time. You'll be in and out of hospitals your whole life.

Fear warped the promise God had given me, making it appear a Trojan horse. It stole the peace and joy I had on surgery day. It lied and took away my sound mind. Eden's first battle had ended; mine was just beginning.

BIG GIRLS DON'T CRY

Our 90-minute drive home from the hospital heralded the next phase of our trial. Eden was not allowed to cry for the next three months. If she cried, the pressure could build up in her brain and cause another aneurysm. Perfect. Our nearly two-year-old was not allowed to cry and oh, she couldn't bump her head either. She had an absorbable plate in her skull to replace the area removed for surgery. On top of everything else, she was on a plethora of different meds that had to be administered by the clock.

Eden turned two during her "no cry" phase. Two! What two-year-old do you know that doesn't test every boundary and cry to manipulate and get their way?

We were overwhelmed.

When things couldn't get any worse, she started getting these crazy dizzy spells where she couldn't even stand. They would come on her quickly. She thought they were hilarious. Her favorite thing to do was run top speed to see how far she could get before falling. Most of the time she could barely stand, and after I chased her down in a blind panic, she would fall over into my lap, unable to sit upright, and laugh and laugh while fear twisted my guts in knots. A few times she ran so fast that she smacked headfirst into a wall before I could catch her. I spent a lot of time warring within myself to keep some form of sanity.

The dizzy spells and her Evil Knievel stunts brought us to the ER in Spokane at least twice. I literally asked for a helmet. The doctor told me it wouldn't do any good because the jarring was the concern.

I was constantly on edge. I understood why but I wish I would have leaned harder into God's promise. I should have listened closer. Our God is faithful. Yet I was so muddled with worry that I couldn't hear Him. My mind was so jumbled with dark thoughts, endless scenarios, and *what ifs* that I couldn't hear His answers to my prayers. What is the opposite of power, love, and a sound mind? Weakness, hate, and confusion.

> *Be sober, be vigilant; because your adversary the devil walks about like a roaring lion, seeking whom he may devour. Resist him, steadfast in the faith, knowing that the same sufferings are experienced by your brotherhood in the world.*
>
> 1 Peter 5:8-9 NKJV

The enemy wants us to hate God. That is where I spent many years during Eden's healing process and afterwards.

I loved God with all my mind but in the depths of my heart, I hated Him without realizing it. I blamed Him for my confusion, my constant state of fear, and the helpless weakling I was becoming.

I didn't see the fear, though. I saw all God allowed as cruelty. I truly thought I loved Him. I felt as if somehow, I'd handle what He was putting me through. I refused to face my anger over having to go through such hardship. I felt hurt and betrayed. I didn't trust God anymore. I was filled with doubt and fear, yet I begged Him to take it all away, knowing He was the only one who could.

I'm sure the devil felt proud in bringing me to a stagnant place in my faith. Stuck in life, I didn't move. I didn't grow. It was as if I was a beleaguered plant and he removed my ability to absorb any nutrients from the soil. Every Word that God spoke in those days was poisoned by toxic fear and doubt, producing bitterness and distrust. If God had to prove His mercy to me, it was in those dark years.

The book of 1 Peter says, "Be sober, be vigilant." I knew it was God that kept me from turning to alcohol. Sometimes I was tempted to, and I know how tempting it is to go to other sources for distraction and induced calm, but *vigilance* prevailed. To be vigilant means to keep careful watch for possible danger or difficulties. Even though I was stagnant and hard-hearted, I still knew God's word, and this saved me from going places I knew I never wanted to go.

I was trying with all my might to keep watch, to maintain with what I knew, but seen through fear-colored glasses, everything in my mind was a danger or difficulty, and the bulwarks God had built in my life were fast eroding under the attack of relentless worry.

We humans tend to run things through the filter of experience rather than the Word of God as we're supposed to. God had given me a Word; one I could align and test with scripture. Had I run my every thought through that Word, fear would have had no place, and peace would have been my portion. Still, it was my lesson to learn, my crucible, my present time of choosing and walking through the valley of death.

The fruit of the spirit is our portion. That's what God longs for us to enjoy. It is when the enemy comes in disguise, a wolf in sheep's clothing, fear lurking as compassion in another mom's question, that the real battle begins. What are we going to believe?

Fear steals our godly portion. We invite things in that we weren't meant to ingest. Today, I understand it: check your filters! Back then, I didn't know I had a filter.

Instead of viewing everything through God's perspective, I struggled through thick muck. But God didn't give up on me, even when I doubted Him. He loves me enough to chase me down and war for me. He continued to surprise me at every turn with things that reminded me of who He is, of who I am. He is worthy of all praise.

Every three months for the first year after Eden's surgery, we went to Spokane for an MRI to see how the valiant girl was healing up. She also had sleep-deprived EEGs and other tests. Often, she required an IV to aestheticize her. I still hate seeing my kids get IV's!

Fear crippled me with every hospital visit. It took all I had to fight the shrieking terrors running through my mind, but you know what? Each time, the tests showed that Eden had healed a little more. In fact, she healed so quickly that it was almost too much for me to process. The doctors were thrilled but I doubted that she was as good as they said she was, even though that is exactly what I was praying for.

My Crucible Moment

When the time came that Eden was allowed to cry again, I couldn't handle it. On the way to the doctor's office, she wasn't allowed to cry, but on the way home, she was safe to wail her heart out. That didn't make sense. I knew they had taken precautions and had given her a proper window for healing, but for me, it was too sudden a step change. Besides, at that point, Eden was used to getting whatever she wanted, whenever she wanted it—anything to keep her from getting upset. Now, faced with the unaccustomed word "No," she could become a royal terror.

I was nervous about what would happen. What would a toddler tantrum bring? Could her brain handle that? What if everything was not ok? What if they missed something? What if there was more damage? *What if...?*

The words rang through my mind with a sickening sting, a poisonous-tip arrow of the enemy piercing my defenseless heart.

Yet Eden got better, day after day. Despite my asking the medical staff a thousand times and receiving ten thousand assurances that she was going to be fine—answers I struggled to accept—she never relapsed, never had any further issues. She finally stopped running into walls for the sheer joy of scaring her mother half to death. As of this writing, she's a healthy, happy 13-year-old who loves unicorns, rainbows and jumping desert canyons on her rocket-powered motorcycle.

Wearing a helmet, of course.

9
Childhood's End

I KNOW NOW WHAT I DIDN'T KNOW THEN. I know what God taught me through that experience—that He is true to His Word. Just as Eden rose from the physical condition that nearly killed her, I eventually rose from the spiritual condition that nearly destroyed my life.

We are not promised an easy ride. We are going to go through hard things in life. It's how we go through them that makes them bearable and life fruitful and enjoyable. Most wouldn't enjoy themselves while their daughter is undergoing life-altering brain surgery, but I did because I had Jesus. It was later, in the aftermath, that I struggled and nearly drowned. Perhaps I was tired, worn down by the initial battle. and ill-prepared for the long siege that lay ahead. Taking the summit turned out to be relatively easy. It was holding the high ground that grew costly, though it was there that I learned what real growth is all about.

Yes, there are going to be things we don't enjoy, things that hurt. But we can have peace and joy in the end if we allow ourselves to see things through God's lens rather than the enemy's distortion. God is our King but He's also a good Father. He holds us when we're in pain. He weeps with us in hardship. And He fights for us when we are overwhelmed with battle.

Many people have said, "God allowed it. He didn't have to. Why would a loving God allow… (fill in the blank)?"

I don't have every answer. But what I do know is we live in a fallen world. A world full of sin. In the beginning, God created Adam and Eve with family in mind. Sin entered in and so did death. Often times, our hurts are a product of other people's sins. God never wanted sin. He wanted a real relationship that was chosen, not forced. People choose. Sometimes their choices negatively affect others.

Other times, it's not sin at all, but a war we can't see going on in the spiritual realm for our souls. Read Job for example. Yes, God allows things, but it was never to destroy Job but rather to prove a point to the enemy. God knew Job. He knew his heart. God didn't want those things to happen to Job, but He allowed them for the bigger picture. He allowed them for the battle to be won. God proved that He knows His children best. He loves us deeply. He longs to bless us. God knew Job would see his children again. God knew where those kids were going. God knew Job loved Him. I don't believe God wanted any of that for Job, but a war was being waged for his soul and God won. The casualties were real. The wake of war is ugly and tragic. But God counted the cost, knew His son Job's abilities, and fought for him in ways perhaps that aren't fully understandable. God also knew what Job's story would do for generations to come.

I am abundantly thankful that I am not Job, but I am also so thankful I have his story and testimony to read and encourage me. What he went through was not only for him but for all those after him. Consider 1 Peter 5:8-9 in the NIV:

> *Be alert and of sober mind. Your enemy the devil prowls around like a roaring lion looking for someone to devour. Resist him, standing firm in the faith, because you know that the family of believers throughout the world is undergoing the same kind of sufferings.*

Notice that "the family of believers throughout the world" is going through difficult things. We are not alone. We have a loving, powerful God and we have each other in the Body of Christ.

But may the God of all grace, who called us to His eternal glory by Christ Jesus, after you have suffered a while, perfect, establish, strengthen, and settle you.

1 Peter 5:10 NKJV

If we make it through, following the advice of the verse to be sober and alert to resist the enemy and be steadfast in our faith, running every thought through God's perspective, we will be perfected, established, strengthened, and settled.

Why do we allow our minds to take us straight to trial and the worst possible outcomes instead of the best possible outcomes? Why do we not turn aside and see, as Moses did with the burning bush, that God will not be consumed? That He has good plans for us. Why do we not hope? Are we preparing for the worst so that if it doesn't happen, we're pleasantly surprised?

How are all of those negative *what ifs* helpful? What fruit do they produce? It's time to retrain our brain. It's time to have faith and trust that God has His best for our lives and for our children!

So circumcise your heart, and stiffen your neck no longer.

Deuteronomy 10:16

Believe God is who He says He is. Stop doing things the way you think they should happen. If you want something different, do things His way. To do that, you have to listen!

Trust the Lord with all your heart, and lean not on your own understanding; in all your ways acknowledge Him, and He shall direct your paths. Do not be wise in your own eyes; fear the Lord and depart from evil.

Proverbs 3:5-7

His ways are better than our ways. Be careful what you say, and what you allow to linger in your mind, for it will settle into your heart.

For out of the abundance of the heart the mouth speaks. A good man out of the good treasure of his heart brings forth good things, and an evil man out of the evil treasure brings forth evil things.

Matthew 12:34b-35

Speak life into your children. Speak truth to them in love.

Death and life are in the power of the tongue, and those who love it will eat of its fruit.

Proverbs 18:21

I am who I am...I AM has sent me to you.

Exodus 3:14

The Lord asked me to write this book. He has sent me to free you from fear, to remind you, teach you and show you that your children are His. Rest knowing that He has good plans for their futures. More than that, that He has eternity in mind. Many of us don't go through life-threatening surgeries or tragedies. I've been through two with my kids now—Eden's brain surgery and two summers ago Judea's appendix burst and we were once again in the children's hospital for a week with moments of uncertainty.

Moses was a great example of insecurity, doubt and also the power of obedience and faith. Sons and daughters, be who you were called to be and allow your children to also! When you see the burning bush of the Lord, turn to it and pay attention. Fire can be alarming, especially in the desert, but it is necessary for you to leave your old ways behind and become a new creation.

I had to live through my battles to become who I am today. I am not finished. We never are. But the fact remains that until we are tested and victorious—note that one does not guarantee the other—our weapons will remain objects of fantasy, the substance of fiery novels and stirring sermons by the weak who run at the slightest provocation. I run sometimes; we all do. But when your baby lies in a twisted heap under a mob of strangers furiously applying all they know to keep him or her alive, you have a choice. Your faith either grows or you remain in the fear, doubt and terror that the enemy offers the faint of heart. I have experienced both—a work in progress, and God brought me through it.

What will your legacy be? What will your story be to the world? What will the fruit of your struggles look like? We all struggle. We are all tested, tried and refined in the fire. What will emerge from your difficulties?

> *These have come so that the proven genuineness of your faith--of greater worth than gold, which perishes even though refined by fire--may result in praise, glory and honor when Jesus Christ is revealed.*
>
> 1 Peter 1:7

Today, I stand on a high mountain pasture, thanking God, and wondering what will come next. I don't know, but I am assured that whatever it is, the warrior I've become in this season of life will be put to the test in the next season.

She will be ready. In Jesus' name, she *will* be ready.

And so will her children.

CHAPTER DISCUSSION QUESTIONS:

1. In what ways have you clenched your fists tightly around your children in fear?

2. What kind of fruit (behavior) are/were you receiving?

3. Ask the Lord to show you areas that you might be deceived, and to shine light and truth to those areas.

4. Were there any areas that you were seeing through filters that were not God's? Ask Him to pour into you, and write it down!

5. What scriptures did He give you to come alongside those things? (if you didn't receive any, ask for some)

6. How do you plan to change the *what ifs* from fear and doubt-based words to faith-based words?

About the Author

MORGAN STIGALL HAS SEVERAL FIERY PASSIONS, but for the sake of sanity and time, we'll mention two: Jesus and parenting well. She has been working with children and youth for 19 years, and in that time has been a nursery pastor, youth pastor, teacher, coach, secretary at a middle school and her most favorite role: a parent.

Morgan and her amazing husband of 17 years, Travis, are raising three awesome children—a boy and two girls: Judea, Eden and Selah.

Morgan knows how hard it is to parent! She's gone through the overwhelmingly amazing, emotional, heart throbbing, exhausting, and sometimes extremely frustrating labor of love herself. She has spent years ministering to not only children and youth but also to their parents. She's studied and draws from a deep well of hands-on experience with all types of children and families including her own! She practices what she preaches and is now reaping the harvest she dreamt of during the years of tilling and preparing, when her kids were tiny babes and tots.

Currently, Morgan is a full-time working mom. Everything she does is with the desire to live a life in obedience to Christ. She longs to set others free, to be an encourager, a truthsayer, and a life speaker. She also loves to spend time with her family, travel, garden, coach, hike and overall be in the sunshine. Two things she loathes: Satan and being cold. (Almost the same thing, right?)

Morgan isn't afraid to go deep into the hard topics and to be vulnerable. She'll speak the truth and uncover lies in a way that might cause you to feel a bit like you're uncovered and stranded in the middle of a field in a lightning storm, but then she'll build you a shelter, give you a warm blanket of hope, some tools for

Childhood's End

survival, a hot cup of sass and humor, and remind you that you can do this life and parenting thing just as well as she can!

Made in the USA
Middletown, DE
17 July 2020